WILLIAM McKINLEY
Stalwart Republican

BY WILLIAM CARL SPIELMAN

Diamond Jubilee History of Carthage College
Introduction to Sources of American History
William McKinley, Stalwart Republican

William McKinley
Stalwart Republican

A BIOGRAPHICAL STUDY

WILLIAM CARL SPIELMAN

Former Professor of History
Carthage College, Carthage, Illinois

EXPOSITION—UNIVERSITY BOOK

EXPOSITION PRESS · NEW YORK

FIRST EDITION

All rights reserved including the right of
reproduction in whole or in part in any form
Copyright, 1954, by William Carl Spielman
Published by the Exposition Press Inc.
386 Fourth Avenue, New York 16, N. Y.
Designed by Morry M. Gropper
Manufactured in the United States of America
Consolidated Book Producers, Inc.
Library of Congress catalog card number: 54-5557

475

Preface

It has been said of William McKinley that he was one of the most obscure major political figures in American history. He has received scant consideration from biographers. Some sketchy partisan lives of McKinley appeared at the time of his first election as President. A more substantial work of two volumes by C. S. Olcott was published in 1916. Other than these, no published life of McKinley seems available.

Since the two-volume work by Olcott much new material of value to the biographer has appeared, most of it in printed form. In organizing and presenting this material I have endeavored to hold to an attitude of sympathetic detachment.

This book was written with a threefold purpose in mind: first, to assign to the subject his place in history amid the social and political conditions of his time; second, to recapture for the reader the personality and character of McKinley the man; third and most important, to present him in the role of protectionist, builder of an empire, political-party leader, and patriot.

W. C. SPIELMAN

Acknowledgments

Grateful acknowledgment for permission to quote from their copyright works is made—

To Appleton-Century-Croft, for *Speeches and Addresses of William McKinley*, edited by J. P. Smith (1893 and 1900)

To Albert and Charles Boni, Inc., for W. F. McCaleb's *Theodore Roosevelt* (1931)

To the City National Bank and Trust Company of Chicago, executor of the Charles G. Dawes estate, for his *Journal of the McKinley Years* (1950)

To Dodd, Mead and Company, for Tyler Dennett's *John Hay* (1934) and for P. C. Jessup's *Elihu Root* (1938)

To Doubleday and Company, for T. B. Mott's *Myron T. Herrick* (1929)

To Harper and Brothers, for R. A. Alger's *The Spanish-American War* (1901), for J. H. Latané's *America as a World Power* (1907), and for H. L. Stoddard's *As I Knew Them: Presidents and Politics From Grant to Coolidge* (1927)

To the Houghton Mifflin Company, for the *Diary and Letters of R. B. Hayes*, edited by C. R. Williams (1922), for J. D. Hicks's *The American Nation: History of the United States From 1865 to the Present* (2d edition, 1949), for Walter Millis' *The Martial Spirit* (1931), for C. S. Olcott's *Life of William McKinley* (1916), and for W. R. Thayer's *Life and Letters of John Hay* (1915)

To Alfred A. Knopf, for Thomas Beer's *Hanna* (1929)

To the Macmillan Company, for W. A. White's *Masks in a Pageant* (1928)

To Daniel Melbane, publisher of the *New Republic*, for Herbert Croly's *M. A. Hanna* (1912)

To Mrs. Ellis P. Oberholtzer, for E. P. Oberholtzer's *History of the United States Since the Civil War* (1937)

To the Ohio State Archeological and Historical Society, for P. D. Jordan's *Ohio Comes of Age, 1873–1900* (1943), and for Everett Walters' *J. B. Foraker* (1948)

To Mr. Leland Powers, for S. L. Powers' *Portraits of a Half Century* (1925)

To G. P. Putnam's Sons, for A. W. Dunn's *From Harrison to Harding* (1922)

To Charles Scribner's Sons, for H. H. Kohlsaat's *From McKinley to Harding: Personal Recollections of Our Presidents* (1923)

Contents

I	Ancestry and Youth	13
II	The Soldier	20
III	Lawyer and Politician	28
IV	From Canton to Washington	35
V	The Drift Toward Tariff Reform	43
VI	The Battle Over Tariff and Surplus	49
VII	Darkening Skies	58
VIII	Governor and Presidential Possibility	63
IX	Master Politician	69
X	A President in the Making	79
XI	Nominated and Elected	87
XII	The McKinley Cabinet	95
XIII	Republican Prosperity	104
XIV	Heading Toward War	111
XV	The War President	124
XVI	Republican Peace and Imperialism	139
XVII	The Path of Empire	148
XVIII	Postwar Diplomacy	159
XIX	The Verdict on Imperialism	167
XX	The McKinleys in Public and Private Life	182
XXI	The Emerging Statesman	191
XXII	Epilogue	199
	Bibliography	207
	Index	211

WILLIAM McKINLEY
Stalwart Republican

CHAPTER I

Ancestry and Youth

The original ancestors of William McKinley, it seems, were a race of sturdy clansmen living in the highlands of Scotland, where they often defended themselves in battle against marauding barons from the lowlands. Scotch chronicles tell of a gallant Highlander known as the Great Findlay, or Finlay, who was killed in the war with England at the Battle of Pinkie in 1547, while carrying the Royal Standard of Scotland.

The Great Findlay, it was stated, was directly though remotely descended from MacDuff, Thane of Fife, immortalized by Shakespeare in his tragedy *Macbeth*. Findlay's older son, William, bore the name MacLanlay of MacKinlay. His sons, it appears, settled in Perthshire, Scotland, and it was the mighty warrior James MacKinlay, their great-grandson, famous in the family annals as James the Trooper, who accompanied the Army of William III of England to Ireland and fought at the Battle of the Boyne in 1690. The Trooper did not return to Scotland, but remained in Ireland and became the founder of the Irish branch of MacKinlays.[1]

---

[1] C. S. Olcott, *Life of McKinley*, Vol. I, pp. 1–3; H. B. Russell, *Lives of McKinley and Hobart*, p. 36.

It seems to be an established fact that the first of William
McKinley's ancestors to migrate to America came from northern
Ireland. This was David McKinley, probably the son of James
the Trooper and known as David the Weaver, who settled in
York County, Pennsylvania. According to one of McKinley's
biographers, David's son John was born and lived in York County
and served in the York County militia in the American Revolution.[2] Two other biographers assert that David had two sons
when he came to America: James, who settled in York County
and founded a northern branch of McKinleys, and William, who
moved south and became the founder of a southern branch by
that name.[3] The three authorities agree that the first McKinley
emigrants to America were Scotch-Irish. William McKinley, it
was said, once met a lady by the same name except that it was
spelled McKinlay. She wondered why the difference in spelling.
He was reported to have replied, "Your ancestors of the Mc-
Kinlay clan came here directly from Scotland and mine came from
the North of Ireland, but we are both of the same stock." [4]

Beginning with James McKinley, founder of the northern
branch of McKinleys, we can trace briefly the American ancestry
of the later President. His great-grandfather David, a son of
James, appears to have fought in the American Revolution as
a Pennsylvania militiaman. David's son James, grandfather of
William McKinley, was a soldier in the War of 1812. So impressed
was he by what he saw of the Ohio country while fighting under
General Harrison that he later located at New Lisbon in Ohio.
There, as the manager of a charcoal furnace for making pig iron,
James McKinley became interested in the flourishing iron industry in eastern Ohio. His son William, father of the President, also
took up iron manufacturing as a business. He too started out by
managing a charcoal furnace and later became a partner of the
firm of iron manufacturers Campbell, McKinley and Dempsey,
located at Niles, Ohio, where in 1843 his seventh child William
Junior was born.[5]

---

[2] Olcott, Vol. I, p. 3.
[3] Russell, pp. 38–39; R. P. Porter, *Life of McKinley*.
[4] Russell, p. 38.
[5] Olcott, Vol. I, pp. 4–5; Russell, p. 40; Porter, p. 22.

Who were the first of William McKinley's maternal ancestors to migrate to America? From what country did they come? Olcott dismisses the subject with a brief statement that the ancestors of Nancy Allison, McKinley's mother, came from Scotland and settled in Westmoreland County, Pennsylvania.[6] The other biographers agree in naming Andrew Rose as the first of McKinley's maternal ancestors to set foot in America, bringing with him his family from Holland, where, it seems, they had fled from England to escape religious persecution. His son, Andrew Rose Jr., was a skilled iron-molder. He too served in the American Revolution, and it was told concerning him that as a soldier he was relieved of military duty after the battle of Monmouth and permitted to return to his home and make much needed ammunition for the patriot armies. Rose resumed his trade of iron-molder after the war.[7] The two families, the McKinleys and the Roses, were united when Mary Rose, daughter of Andrew Jr., married James McKinley and subsequently became the grandmother of William McKinley.[8] Her son, William McKinley, Sr., married Nancy Allison, whose forebears, according to one of McKinley's biographers, were originally from England and after coming to America settled in Virginia. Some of the Allisons later moved to Greene County, Pennsylvania, where Abner Allison, father of Nancy and grandfather of William McKinley, was born. Nancy Allison's mother was Ann Campbell, whom Abner Allison married in 1798, and who, according to that same writer, was of a Scotch-German family.[9]

The ancestral background of William McKinley was industrial. One great-grandfather, Andrew Rose was, as we noted, a skilled iron-molder by trade. Two of Andrew's sons worked with McKinley senior in his iron foundry in New Lisbon, Ohio. A third son and McKinley were interested in the iron industry in Mercer County, Pennsylvania.[10] A great-grandfather of William McKinley, David McKinley, as has been noted, was an iron

---

[6] Olcott, Vol. I, p. 5.
[7] Russell, pp. 41–42; Porter pp. 23–24.
[8] *Ibid.*
[9] Russell, p. 42.
[10] Russell, pp. 40–44.

molder at the time of the Revolution. His grandfather, James McKinley, after moving to Ohio, engaged in the making of pig iron; and William McKinley's father became active in the iron industry of eastern Ohio. Since iron manufacturing had in a sense become a tradition in the McKinley family, it would scarcely seem surprising if William McKinley's ideas on the subject of the tariff and protection were later molded to some extent by his ancestral background.

Young McKinley's early life was spent in several places, the first being the hamlet of Niles, Ohio, where he was born. Small as it was, Niles could boast of a rolling mill, a blast furnace, a forge, a grist mill, three churches, a school, and three stores. Except for stagecoach connections with Pittsburgh, the town was much isolated and dependent on itself for its existence. It was not until 1848 that Niles had rail connection with Dayton and Sandusky.

The McKinleys lived on the second floor of a long, two-story frame dwelling that stood on a corner of the main thoroughfare, over which trickled the life of the community. The first floor was mainly occupied by a country store.

The seventh of nine children, young William early grew familiar with the give-and-take that goes with being brought up in a large family. As one of the younger children he was no doubt obliged to submit to the attention and supervision imposed by older brothers and sisters, and perhaps he learned to put up with them gracefully, if not willingly. The two older sisters, Anna and Helen, seem to have exerted much wholesome influence during his formative years. With the possible exception of his mother, no woman did more to mold McKinley's character in early life than his spinster sister Anna, a seasoned schoolteacher of many years. Helen, though older than William, was still young enough to be a companionable playmate.

After passing the first nine years of his life in Niles, young McKinley moved with his family to Poland in Mahoning County, near Youngstown. Poland was a more populous place, situated near coal and iron mines. What perhaps counted most with the McKinleys was the educational advantages the town offered for their children. In Poland was a seminary occupying a newly built three-story brick building. Under the control of the Methodist Episcopal church, it had a good teaching staff and furnished superior educational opportunities. McKinley attended the seminary several years and acquired from it much of his formal training in mathematics, English, and the classical languages. Of the teachers at the seminary, a Miss Blakeley, a graduate of Oberlin College, left a strong impress on the student in his early years there. McKinley later paid tribute to her influence as a teacher.

While a student at Poland, William McKinley took a leading part in the Everett Literary and Debating Society. He helped organize it and was its first president. The Everett Society had a room on the third floor of the seminary building, where it met regularly each week to conduct spirited debates on current questions of public interest.[11]

One of the less formal but by no means less potent educational forces in McKinley's youth was his home environment. His biographers agree that the McKinley home was a center of mental and cultural stimulus. One of them speaks of the family collection of books, which included such standard works as Hume's *History of England*, Gibbon's *Decline and Fall of the Roman Empire*, the early writings of Charles Dickens, and a volume of Shakespeare.[12] The McKinleys subscribed to several magazines and to Greeley's *Weekly New York Tribune*. Daily oral reading was customary. After the evening meal, each member of the family circle would in turn read aloud while the others sat and listened.

Religion was another potent factor. William and Nancy McKinley were both devout Methodists. The older children were also members of the Methodist church. While attending a religious revival, young William and sister Sarah united with the Methodist Episcopal Church in Poland. Thereafter he continued to be a loyal Methodist to the end of his days. After uniting with the church he came into close contact with the minister, the Reverend W. F. Day, from whom McKinley received instruction in Old Testament Hebrew, and he was a member of a Bible

[11] Olcott, Vol. I, p. 20; Russell, p. 56.
[12] Russell, p. 49.

class.[13] These contacts may well have been of lasting spiritual value to the lad in his teens.

From what has previously been stated we can readily surmise that young McKinley was of a rather serious turn of mind and fond of books and study. Quite early, he acquired the habit of spending much time in reading and study, often staying up until late hours, "burning the midnight oil." [14] This is in keeping with the fact that in later life McKinley was known for the close and intensive application that he gave to the study of economic and social problems. It should be noted, however, that he was never a great reader, nor did he acquire a wide familiarity with books.

As a youth McKinley was of sturdy build and apparently enjoyed normal health. There were occasional exceptions. In the fall of 1860, while he was a junior at Alleghany College, Meadville, Pennsylvania, his career as a student was cut short by severe illness. He was forced to give up his studies and return home. His illness, as a biographer had suggested, may have resulted from too close application to his studies and not enough physical exercise.[15]

Like most normal youths, McKinley at times doubtless felt the lure of the great outdoors. Like others, he went hunting, fishing, and skating when these sports were in season. But we may question whether they had as much appeal for him as for his companions. He could not swim, and on one occasion this deficiency nearly cost him his life.[16] In one sport, however, young McKinley probably surpassed all his companions: he was an accomplished horseman. His skill in handling mounts proved highly valuable to him as a soldier in the Civil War.

The McKinley family was one of limited means. William and Nancy McKinley, however, gave their children such advantages as lay within their humble means and, most important of all, provided for their education. When William Junior came back from Alleghany College, he supported himself by teaching in a

---

13 Russell, pp. 55–56; Olcott, Vol. I, pp. 18–19.
14 Russell, p. 57.
15 Russell, p. 58.
16 Olcott, Vol. I, p. 9.

neighboring country school. He also worked for a time as a clerk in the Poland post office. When he returned from the war at the age of twenty-two and decided to prepare for the law, his family could apparently give him no assistance. But he received a substantial loan from a personal friend, R. L. Walker of Poland, which made it possible to devote himself entirely to reading law and later to attend the law school at Albany, New York. For many years after McKinley was admitted to the bar this loan remained unpaid. During McKinley's first term as governor of Ohio he endorsed a note for Walker for $5,000, which happened to be the sum of the original loan. The note was held for collection by a Cleveland bank. When this came to the attention of some of the Governor's friends, they quietly raised enough money among themselves to pay off the debt that he had been owing Walker since his youth. The tendency to accept largess from others appears to have followed McKinley to a certain extent through life.[17]

McKinley apparently developed in early life an urgent fondness for politics. He probably acquired a taste for politics and political discussion from his father. The ambition to carve out a political career grew in him, especially after he had realized his first important success, his election to Congress in 1876. Many an American youth of an ambitious turn has had visions of attaining to and holding high public office. Many youths may even have dreamed at times of becoming President some day. McKinley's youthful ambition to be President seems to have amounted to something more substantial than visions and dreams. It rested upon a virtual certainty formed in his mind in early youth that he would beyond a doubt sometime see his ambition realized.[18]

---

[17] J. T. Flynn, *Men of Wealth*, pp. 401–2.

[18] S. L. Powers, *Portraits of a Half Century*, p. 164: "I have never been in doubt since I was old enough to think intelligently that I would sometime be made President. Things are now taking shape in a manner that my ambition will be realized four years hence." (From a statement by McKinley in 1892; reprinted by permission of Leland Powers.)

CHAPTER II

The Soldier

As in hundreds of communities in the land, the people of Poland were electrified by the news from Fort Sumter that came flashing over the wires. The whole town turned out, to judge by the crowd in front of the Sparrow House. The streets were lined with the horses and conveyances of farmers coming in from the country. A fife-and-drum corps led by a Mexican War veteran added to the excitement. Poland's leading lawyer, C. E. Glidden, known for his eloquence, addressed the crowd and urged the young men to enlist immediately in response to Lincoln's call for volunteers.

Among the spectators were young William McKinley and his cousin William McKinley Osborne. They listened to Judge Glidden, but decided not to enlist immediately. They drove to Youngstown to watch the company of recruits from Poland leave for Camp Chase, near Columbus. On his return, McKinley told his mother of his desire to enlist, and having gained her consent, he went to Camp Chase for that purpose.

At Camp Chase he and others from Poland learned that the quotas of enlistments for three months from Ohio were already filled. Were they willing to enlist for three years? Otherwise, there was no choice, they were told, but to return home. Not only leader, was to be pitted against the great Confederate cavalry-man. For that purpose he was placed in command of a consolidated military division which included the Army of West Virginia under General Crook. At the head of the second division of Crook's army was General Hayes.

Taking the initiative as was his custom, Sheridan quickly moved against Early. But the Confederate general's troops were so firmly stationed at Opequam that for a whole month Sheridan would not risk an attack. Then, apparently acting on information from a Union sympathizer in Winchester that some of Early's forces had been transferred to Richmond, Sheridan decided to advance.[6]

The attack was successfully executed under devastating rifle and artillery fire from the Confederates, who were pushed back and at length retreated. During the battle McKinley, military aide to General Crook, was in the saddle much of the time, riding about carrying dispatches from his commanding officer. Instead of a written message he was given oral orders to General Duval of the second division, directing him to move his command to the right of the sixth corps. Though McKinley was not told the route Duval should take, he was not unprepared when asked about it. "I would go up the creek," he is reported to have answered. Not satisfied, Duval refused to move without definite written orders. To return to General Crook for further orders was impossible under the circumstances. Consequently McKinley decided to take the responsibility on himself. Saluting the officer, he ordered him to move his division up the ravine. It was a precarious maneuver, but since it was successfully completed and Duval's division managed to reunite with Crook's forces, it reflected credit on the young military aide for his coolness, daring, and sound judgment. A man less inclined to assume responsibility would probably have been criticized for not acting as McKinley did to carry out his mission.

Sheridan followed up his victory at Opequam with another at

---

[6] F. A. Burr and R. J. Hinton, *Life of General Philip Sheridan*, p. 197, for the story of Rebecca Wright, the young Quaker who, being loyal to the Union, gave the information to Sheridan.

Fisher's Hill, where Early had taken another strong position. Realizing the disadvantage of his own position, the intrepid Union commander ordered General Crook to make a flank attack under cover of the mountains while the main army engaged the enemy's attention by a frontal assault. Crook's movement was a complete success. The Confederates were taken by surprise and, after being routed in a sharp battle, continued to retreat southward, while Sheridan led his cavalry in close pursuit.

Early, avoiding all attempts by Sheridan to draw him into open battle, eluded his pursuer for an entire month. Sheridan then took up an apparently strong position at Cedar Creek, some seventy miles south of Winchester, and went to Washington to attend a conference of war officers. On the evening of October 18 he returned from Washington and, having assured himself that his presence at Cedar Creek would not be necessary until the next day, remained in Winchester for the night. Toward morning he was awakened by heavy cannonading to the south. Mounting his black charger, Sheridan set out for Cedar Creek at top speed. Making a detour around the village of Newtown, he met Captain McKinley of General Crook's staff. From him he learned of the unexpected attack by Early's troops on Crook's men as they lay asleep in camp. Overwhelmed by the enemy's numbers, many Union soldiers had fallen and the remainder had broken ranks and were in flight.[7]

McKinley at once spread the news of Sheridan's arrival. By that time his appearance had so electrified the dispirited troops that they quickly re-formed and with cheers and shouts returned to the charge. The result was one of the most amazing victories recorded in history.

Cedar Creek was also the last engagement in which McKinley took part. When General Hancock succeeded General Crook, the young aide was transferred to Hancock's staff. At the close of the

---

[7] P. H. Sheridan, *Personal Memoirs*, Vol. I, pp. 81–82. In a letter to his son dated November 4, 1864, Hayes wrote: "He [McKinley] has not been wounded but everyone admires him as one of the bravest and finest young officers in the army. He has had two or three horses shot under him." (*Diary and Letters of R. B. Hayes*, Vol. II, p. 534; reprinted by permission of the Houghton Mifflin Company.)

war McKinley was on the staff of General S. S. Carroll, in command of the Veterans' Reserve Corps, under whom he served as assistant adjutant-general of the First Division. He was mustered out of service on July 26, 1865. When he returned to his home in Poland, he carried with him a document bearing the signature A. Lincoln. It was his commission as brevet major of the United States Volunteers, "for gallant and meritorious services at the battles of Opequam, Cedar Creek, and Fisher's Hill."[8]

---

[8] Olcott, Vol. I, p. 53.

CHAPTER III

Lawyer and Politician

When it came to deciding upon a career, the twenty-two-year-old war veteran had three possibilities from which to choose. For a commissioned army officer the life of a military man was one. Such a career, particularly in time of peace, offered a life of comparative ease, comfort, and security. Moreover, for a Regular Army man there was also the opportunity of promotion. It is quite possible that young McKinley may have discussed the subject with the superior officers to whose staff he was attached during the war, some of whom may have favored the army as a career while others opposed it. However alluring life in the army may have been to some veterans just returned from the war, it apparently made no appeal to McKinley.

Business offered another opportunity for the young soldier. The era of American industrialization set in as the war ended, and American industry made giant strides in the postwar years and over the last quarter of the nineteenth century. McKinley's life ran parallel with this industrialization. For many young men of his generation the business world with its opportunities for profits would have been very tempting. Across the horizon of coming personalities in business, a number of the great captains of industry were already casting their shadows: Rockefeller in the oil industry, Vanderbilt in transportation, Carnegie in steel, Armour in meat-packing. But McKinley had his mind fixed on the legal profession, and for this his fondness for books and habits of study, together with his ability to speak in public, seemed to qualify him. That for an ambitious young lawyer the law was often a gateway to politics and public life probably occurred to him too.

Over against these advantages there were certain disadvantages which must be carefully weighed. Among these were the time and money required to prepare himself for the law and the lean years to be endured before he could build up a lucrative law practice. The pros and cons involved in making a decision were probably discussed at length with friends and members of his family. If so, we can be sure that he was given a good deal of advice, some of it sound, some of it not so sound, all of it free.

Of those with whom McKinley conferred, it seems likely that in deciding to study law he was most influenced by members of his family, and once he had made the decision, it was probably his older sister Anna who inspired him to make the sacrifices necessary to achieve his ambition. He began to read law under C. E. Glidden, who had recently been elected judge of Mahoning County and whose office was in Youngstown. To the judge's office the young law student went to recite what he had read in the law books. After a year or more of this, it was decided that he should attend the Albany Law School for a term from September, 1866. He was in Albany until the spring of 1867, and when he returned was admitted to the bar in Warren, Ohio.

McKinley decided to practice at Canton, county seat of Stark County, a town of about five thousand surrounded by a rich, prosperous countryside and with excellent possibilities for industrial growth. Politically, Canton and Stark counties were predominantly Democratic.

McKinley's first legal business, strangely enough, dealt with a case in court. One day Judge George W. Belden, whose office was in the same building as McKinley's, asked him to try a case for him, the case to come up the next day. McKinley hesitated at first because he had not tried a case in court before. But when Belden insisted he consented to take it. He remained in his office all night preparing his argument, and next day appeared in court and won the case.[1] There had been no understanding with Belden as to the fee he was to receive, and McKinley was much surprised when he was paid twenty-five dollars out of a retainer received by Belden. Soon after this McKinley became Belden's partner and continued so until the Judge's death in 1870. It was a very fortunate arrangement, for as Judge Belden's partner, McKinley stepped into a well-established and profitable law practice.[2]

Meantime his ability to speak well in public brought him to the attention of Republican politicians. In 1867, when the proposed Fifteenth Amendment to prevent a state from denying Negroes the right to vote was up for ratification, McKinley undertook to stump Stark County urging that it be ratified. But Negro suffrage was unpopular in Ohio and notably so in Stark County, with its predominantly Democratic population. For the young lawyer to go before the people and argue for such a measure was in itself an act of courage. Although he was unable to overcome the prejudices of his hearers, McKinley's skill as a speaker and his able presentation of the subject of Negro suffrage created a favorable impression even with his political opponents. The same year McKinley also campaigned for his former commander, General Hayes, who was making his first bid for popular support as the Republican candidate for governor of Ohio. The political odds against Hayes were heavy, but he succeeded in carrying the state by a small plurality.[3]

In 1869 young McKinley made his first appearance as a candidate for political honors. Republicans of Stark County decided that year to nominate him for prosecuting attorney. The Democratic candidate, W. A. Lynch, known all over the county as a brilliant lawyer, seemed almost certain to be elected by an over-

---

[1] Olcott, Vol. I, p. 59.
[2] Olcott, Vol. I, pp. 60–61.
[3] Olcott, Vol. I, pp. 72–74.

whelming vote. To the most casual observer McKinley's defeat seemed almost inevitable. Battle-scarred veterans of the political game would doubtless not have conceded him a fighting chance to win. An apparently hopeless contest, however, turned out to be a remarkable triumph. For his astonishing success at the polls the young lawyer deserved full credit, for he owed his election to his vigorous canvass of Stark County and to the reputation that he was making for himself in the public eye as a serious student of government and politics and as a man of high and incorruptible morals. Thus, at the early age of twenty-six, McKinley took his first step up the ladder to political fame.

McKinley's victory in 1869, together with a very commendable record as prosecuting attorney, pointed to him as the logical candidate for the office two years later. He was again given the nomination by the Republican County Convention. The democrats again picked Lynch as their ablest candidate. Having profited by his previous experience and with his party organization firmly behind him, he exerted himself to the utmost to break down his opponent's political strength. He was successful, though he won the election by a narrow majority of only one hundred and forty-three votes.[4]

The next campaign in which McKinley took part was the spirited one of 1875. Governor Allen, the Democratic candidate, was making an energetic bid for re-election. His record was a good one, and on that basis his chances of re-election seemed excellent. To prevent it the Republicans nominated Hayes for the third time. He had twice before been governor and was regarded in Republican circles as the foremost political figure in Ohio. The issues of the campaign, more national than local, dealt with the money question. The Republicans advocated a return to sound money, by which they meant coined money or specie currency. They declared themselves for the Resumption Act recently passed by Congress, under which outstanding greenbacks or legal-tender notes were to be redeemed by a gold reserve to be created by the Secretary of the Treasury by January

---

[4] Olcott, Vol. I, p. 76.

1, 1879. The Democrats called for paper currency, condemned the resumption principle, and insisted that greenback notes be continued in circulation and even expanded in volume to meet business needs. Governor Allen symbolized the "soft money" theory of the Democrats, while Hayes, who branded this as "heresy," made himself a leading champion of Republican doctrine on currency.

In a statewide speaking tour McKinley actively assisted in rallying the soldier vote of the state in support of Hayes. His uncompromising support of the Resumption Act for the retirement of legal-tender notes is both interesting and significant because of his stand in Congress on the money question and his position on the same issue as a Presidential candidate twenty years later.[5]

Hayes was elected governor for the third time in 1875. Ohio Republicans were elated and felt that they had good reasons for elation. They felt confident that Hayes, if nominated for the Presidency by the Republican National Convention in 1876, would carry his state and lead his party to national victory.

For William McKinley the year 1876 turned out to be an eventful one. In June he appeared in court as counsel in a case attracting widespread attention. It grew out of a strike among soft-coal miners in the Tuscarawas Valley coal mines in the spring. The miners, who suffered severely from the hard times of the 1870's, had gone on strike against the demand of their employers that their wages be reduced. In striking the miners disregarded the advice of their union leaders to submit their differences with the operators to arbitration. The situation grew worse when strike-breakers from Cleveland were brought in by the operating companies. Violence resulted, and the manager of a mine owned by Rhodes and Company was attacked and nearly killed. Other mines of the company were seized by the strikers and set on fire. Governor Hayes, when appealed to, sent a company of militia to the scene, and order was finally restored.

A large number of strikers were arrested and sent to Canton

---

[5] Olcott, Vol. I, pp. 77–78.

to await trial. So inflamed was public sentiment against the miners that no lawyer in the community could be found to defend them in court until McKinley agreed to take the case. He handled it so effectively that all but one of the twenty-three miners indicted for trial were acquitted, the one convicted defendant being sentenced to the penitentiary for three years. Having thus shown his sympathy for the mineworkers, McKinley gave additional proof of his sympathetic attitude toward them by refusing to take any payment from them for his services.[6]

The trial was significant, too, in other ways. It served to bring together for the first time three rising young Ohioans who were destined to reach high rank in their respective spheres. Mark Hanna was a leading member of Rhodes and Company, one of the largest coal and iron firms in northern Ohio. As an employer of striking miners who had destroyed some of the mine property of his company, he could scarcely be expected to look with composure on the wholesale acquittal of the miscreants that resulted from McKinley's able pleading of their case. Whatever his attitude may have been at the time, it apparently was not a determining factor in shaping Hanna's subsequent personal relations with McKinley. Hanna in time became McKinley's foremost political adviser and intimate friend.

The attorneys for the coal operators happened to be the law firm Lynch and Day. Its senior member was the man who had twice been McKinley's opponent in the contest for district attorney of Stark County. The junior member, W. R. Day, later grew to be another close and fast friend, and after McKinley's elevation to the White House Day was appointed Secretary of State.[7]

Shortly after the trial McKinley was nominated Republican candidate for Congress by the congressional convention of the eighteenth district, composed at the time of Stark, Columbiana, Mahoning, and Carroll counties. He had already announced himself as a candidate before the convention met. Three other aspirants for the Republican nomination were in the field, all of

---

[6] Herbert Croly, *M. A. Hanna*, pp. 91 ff.; Olcott, Vol. I, pp. 78–80.
[7] Olcott, Vol. I, p. 80.

them older and more seasoned.[8] To the surprise of many, the nomination went to McKinley on the first ballot. Thereupon the youthful candidate bent his energies toward attaining a goal that he had long set his heart on, a seat in Congress—a goal well within reach of a man of his qualities. The result was a splendid victory. McKinley defeated his Democratic adversary by a thirty-three-hundred-vote majority. His election was the beginning of a distinguished career in Congress lasting more than fourteen years.

McKinley's election in 1876 also proved to be the beginning of an unbroken career in public office extending over a quarter century. The same year, moreover, marked a turning point in the married life of William McKinley and his young wife Ida. In that year the older of their children, Katherine, or Katie, died at the tender age of four. The other child, Ida by name, had died in infancy three years earlier. The death of Mrs. McKinley's mother, to whom her daughter was greatly attached, occurred the same year. The loss of the mother and both children brought deep sorrow to the McKinleys and especially to Mrs. McKinley, whose health was so impaired by shock and grief that she became an invalid for the rest of her life.

---

[8] They were L. D. Woodworth, representing the district at the time; Joseph Frease, well-known judge in Canton; and Josiah Hartsell, editor of the Canton *Repository* (Olcott, Vol. I, pp. 80–81).

From Canton to Washington

The new Congressman from Canton went to Washington in October, 1877, to take his seat in the Forty-fifth Congress, which was meeting in special session. General Hayes, McKinley's commander in the late war, was in the White House. Hayes had been inaugurated March 4, 1877. Only two days before, the electoral commission chosen by Congress to canvass the disputed electoral votes of 1876 had submitted a strictly partisan report declaring Hayes elected over Tilden by one electoral vote. Only then was the frightening suspense and excitement that had gripped the nation for four months brought to an end.

When McKinley took his seat in Congress the political scene in Washington was changing. Southern reconstruction was receding in the background. The scandalous Republican carpetbag governments imposed on the Southern states had collapsed in all but three of them: Florida, South Carolina, and Louisiana. In Florida the inauguration of a Democratic governor early in 1877 marked the end of carpetbag rule in that state. In the other states Republican carpetbaggers maintained themselves in power only by the help of Federal troops stationed at their capitols, without whose support their regime would also end. In the face of fierce criticism Hayes ordered the troops withdrawn from South Carolina and Louisiana and permitted Southern Democratic officials to take over the vacancies left by the ousted carpetbaggers. The "solid South" of the Democratic party was then restored and the last trace of political reconstruction swept away.

The challenging issues before the Hayes administration were civil-service reform and the currency. To the first Hayes gave full support. Under President Grant the cause of civil-service reform had languished and all but perished for want of support. A civil-service commission, with George W. Curtis as its head, was rendered powerless when Congress refused to vote the funds needed to keep it going. Hayes aimed to secure an efficient commission, but in the meantime he contented himself with issuing instructions for the executive departments to follow. A few department heads complied, but the rest calmly ignored the President's orders, and Congress showed no willingness at all to respond to his request for a competent civil-service commission. Hayes therefore appointed competent and honest officials wherever possible without regard to politics. This soon brought him into an open clash with Republican wheelhorses in Congress, who refused to approve his removal of a notorious politician as Collector of the Port of New York and the appointment in his place of a man of known integrity and efficiency.

On the currency his stand was exactly that held by him as governor. Hayes was for "sound money." He advocated restricting the volume of greenback notes in circulation and making them convertible into gold from a gold reserve to be created under the Resumption Act of 1875. To insure the carrying out of this law Hayes appointed John Sherman, leading sponsor of the measure, Secretary of the Treasury. As required, Sherman, with the full backing of the President, sold bonds for gold and thus amassed a gold reserve of one hundred million dollars in anticipation of the resumption of specie payments on January 1, 1879.

Since 1873, when Congress had demonetized the silver dollar, the value of silver bullion had been dropping. The drop was due to the vast quantity of the white metal thrown on the market after the discovery of new silver mines and to improved methods of mining and refining silver ore. Owners of silver mines, however, blamed the demonetization of the silver dollar for the drop in value and spoke of it as "the crime of 1873." Soon there arose, first among the mine-owners and producers and then among the debtor, farmer, and planter classes in the West and South, a powerful demand for Congress to remonetize silver and to enact the free and unlimited purchase and coinage of silver.

In response to this demand the Bland bill was introduced in the special session of Congress in which McKinley had just taken his seat. The bill provided that the government purchase all silver bullion brought to its mints and have it coined into standard silver dollars that should be legal tender in payment of all debts, public and private. The bill passed the House, but was amended in the Senate to the effect that the government should purchase not all silver brought to it, but between two and four million dollars' worth each month. Thus the Bland bill of the House became the Bland-Allison bill of the Senate. Vetoed by the President, it was repassed and became law.

Each time the bill came before the House McKinley voted on it. He voted for the original Bland bill; he voted for the amended Bland-Allison measure; and his third vote helped to pass the measure over Hayes's veto.[1] How did this record square with the sound-money ideas advanced by McKinley in his Ohio campaign two years before?

When McKinley argued for the special Resumption Act during his tour of Ohio, he put himself on record against a further expansion of greenback currency. Greenback notes, as he explained, were to be made redeemable in gold dollars paid from a gold reserve. Thus he helped to puncture the Ohio idea of Governor Allen of an inflated paper currency. His votes on the Bland-Allison bill make clear that as congressman he had shifted his position, for in supporting that measure McKinley declared himself for an expansion of the nation's silver currency by pouring into it a stream of new silver dollars coined from monthly purchases of from two to four million dollars' worth of silver. His vote for the original Bland bill was an unqualified vote for free

---

[1] Olcott, Vol. I, p. 197.

silver. With this exception McKinley, it may be said, held stead-
fastly to the limited-purchase-and-coinage principle of the Bland-
Allison Act.[2]

It would be unreasonable to expect the young thirty-four-year-
old congressman to foresee what many an older man in public
life did not foresee: that the Bland-Allison Act which he voted to
place on the statute books would eventually sweep most of the
country's gold out of circulation and put the country practically
on a silver basis. Neither would it be reasonable to accuse
McKinley of being shortsighted when later he voted for the
Silver Purchase Act, which, with its vicious chain of treasury
notes, almost pumped dry the precious gold-reserve fund set
aside for the sole purpose of stabilizing depreciated greenbacks.

It was not on the currency question, however, but on the tariff
that McKinley built his reputation as a lawmaker in Congress.
When he entered Congress his knowledge of the tariff was
doubtless meager and inconsequential. Then, as a result of self-
education on the subject, he grew in time to be a recognized expert on the tariff and a leading protectionist spokesman in Congress.

The initial impulse of his protectionist career was probably
supplied soon after the Forty-fifth Congress convened in regular
session. Steel and iron manufacturers from his district in Ohio
sent him petitions to lay before the House. They were petitioning
against any revision of the existing tariff schedules until an investigation had been made to determine the kind of tariff that would
best restore general prosperity. These petitions McKinley presented on December 10, 1877. They were not likely to be taken
very seriously by the Democratic members, who were in the
majority. Other congressmen were also presenting similar petitions from their constituents.

----

[2] In voting for the Silver Purchase Act of 1890 McKinley practically supported the same principle, but in this case payment for the 4,500,000 ounces
of silver bought each month was to be made in Treasury notes redeemable
either in silver or in gold. When speaking for this bill he declared himself
against free silver and the bimetallic standard unless it were adopted by
other countries under international agreement. (*Speeches and Addresses*,
1893, pp. 454–55.)

Meantime the Ways and Means Committee was at work on a new tariff bill. Its chairman, Fernando Wood of New York, reported the bill on March 26, and it was brought up for consideration in the House on April 9. The purpose of the bill as stated by Wood was to revive the country's depressed economy, and it proposed to do this by a reduction of existing tariff duties by an average of 15 per cent. The actual number of dutiable articles, he explained, was to be reduced from 2,272 to 575.[3]

Practically all the high tariff duties of the Civil War were still in effect at this time. In some instances, such as those on wool, coffee, marble, and nickel, the duties had been made even higher. The tariff of 1872 contained reductions, but most of them were restored in 1875, including an increased duty of 25 per cent on sugar and molasses, so that the former high war rates were practically reinstated. Tariff reformers insisting on lowered duties asserted that the public was paying on over 4,000 dutiable articles, whereas only 400 were duty-free. In 1881 tariff receipts of the government reached a new high. Two-thirds of these receipts from the tariff were collected on imports of sugar and molasses, wool and woolen goods, iron and steel products, silk and cotton manufactures, wines and liquors. Continuation of the high war tariff could scarcely be justified on the ground that the beneficiaries were infant industries needing protection. Most of them were already well established. Neither could the high rates be defended on the old plea that the treasury needed more revenue, for by 1880 a surplus of $68,000,000 had developed, which grew to $100,000,000 within the next year.[4] The presence of such a surplus in the Treasury was a constant temptation to Congress to fritter it away on costly and wasteful public projects.

Economists and students who looked at the tariff objectively were urging that it be revised for other reasons. It tended for one thing, they pointed out, to slow down foreign trade, because other countries could not buy our raw products unless permitted to

---

[3] Olcott, Vol. I, pp. 129–31. This was probably an exaggeration. Tariff schedules from 1867 to 1883 never contained more than 1,600 enumerated articles, of which about 400 were free.

[4] E. E. Sparks, *National Development*, pp. 282 ff.

sell us their manufactures. Furthermore, the American people, they maintained, and particularly ordinary people with limited incomes, were burdened by the cost of high-priced tariff-protected necessities.

McKinley, however, was in full accord with the wishes of his Ohio constituents. In the next four or five months he made an intensive study of the tariff, so that he would be prepared when the new bill was brought up for debate to take the floor and speak against it. On April 15, exactly six months after taking his seat, the gentleman from Canton delivered his first speech. It was replete with factual matter obtained from his study and contained an imposing array of figures and statistics to buttress his protectionist contentions.

He attacked the new bill by asserting that there was no need for altering or revising the existing law. To alter it when the manufacturing interests of the country were in such depression and paralysis would mean disaster. Moreover, he contended, there was no national demand for such a change as the new bill proposed. On the contrary, manufacturers, farmers, mechanics, laboring men, and miners were united in opposing the measure. Why change the present tariff under which many new enterprises had been started, involving the investment of tremendous sums of capital in buildings and factories all over the land? "In my own district," he said, "with its wealth of mineral resources, its factories, machine shops, mills and furnaces, the disaster which must result from the passage of the pending bill can not be estimated. The rich coal mines abounding in the counties of Stark, Mahoning, and Columbiana will be forced to diminish their production and the miners driven into other avenues of labor already overcrowded. The mills and furnaces, factories and machine shops situated in these counties are famous for their iron and steel and agricultural implements. They have struggled with unyielding courage through the panic of 1873 and the distressing years that have followed, and even the meager wages now paid are keeping thousands of families from actual want. All of them must, I am assured if the present bill becomes law, put out their fires, while the potteries of East Liverpool which are employing

and business-like examination and revision of the tariff by competent civilians who shall be Americans favorable to the American system."[3]

On the other hand, he saw reasons for questioning the setting-up of a commission, since the present tariff laws contained "excrescences" and "incongruities" and other wrongs that should be corrected immediately rather than retained until a commission could report on them and Congress take action. Moreover, he regarded the commission idea as being a hazardous thing. It would mean delegating to another agency powers and responsibility that belong only to Congress, and although a commission could gather much important and valuable information, the sources it used would be the same ones available to Congress and to the Ways and Means Committee.[4] Nevertheless he would favor creating a commission authorized to report to Congress, leaving Congress to accept what was good in the report and reject the rest.

Although all nine members of the tariff commission were protectionists, it reported a schedule of tariff rates amounting to an average reduction of 20 per cent from existing rates. The commission's report was referred by the Senate to its Finance Committee and by the House to its Ways and Means Committee, a majority of whom were Republican protectionists. On January 23, 1883, while the House was in Committee of the Whole to consider the bill prepared by the Ways and Means Committee, McKinley rose to speak for the measure. He called attention to the revisions it contained. Duties were reduced in every schedule except those on cotton and cotton goods, earthenware, and glassware. The total sum, he estimated, would be over $23,000,000. In making these reductions, the Ways and Means Committee had closely followed the report of the tariff commission, whose members McKinley characterized as "intelligent, conscientious, ca-

---

[3] *Speeches and Addresses*, p. 72.

[4] *Speeches and Addresses*, p. 73. Now that he was a member of the Ways and Means and realized its importance in initiating and framing laws on the tariff, the speech makes it evident that McKinley was rather reluctant that the committee should surrender this power to an outside executive agency.

pable men and peers of the best men on the floor of this House." [5]
Some rates, he explained, were raised above those of the commission's report, but in a large majority of cases the reductions
proposed in the report had been accepted, and in a considerable
number of instances duties lower than those proposed were
recommended by the Ways and Means Committee. He was for
the new bill, too, because it would be easy to administer and
equitable to American interests.

The tariff bills as passed by both houses were referred to a
conference committee, which greatly altered them. In fact, the
committee exceeded its authority and played fast and loose with
the schedules as submitted. The rates were boosted almost up to
the old tariff levels. After much wrangling, the conference committee report was voted through and translated into a practically
new tariff law on March 3, 1883, the very last day of the Forty-
seventh Congress. Labeled "the Mongrel Tariff," it was very
unsatisfactory to many protectionists and bitterly disappointing
to tariff reformers. [6]

The Mongrel Tariff intensified the drift toward tariff reform,
especially in the Democratic party. Soon after Congress convened in December, 1883, the House, now under Democratic
sway, instead of selecting Randall, who had been Speaker three
times, chose for that post a low-tariff advocate, J. G. Carlisle of
Kentucky. For chairman of the Ways and Means Committee another tariff reformer, W. R. Morrison of Illinois, was named.
Morrison lost no time in getting his committee to work on a bill
for downward revision of the tariff. As reported by Morrison in
March, 1884, the bill proposed to make a horizontal cut of 20 per
cent on almost all dutiable articles.

On April 30 McKinley again took the floor in a speech against
the measure. He began by warning the House that this was only
the first step by Democratic members of the Ways and Means

---

[5] *Speeches and Addresses*, pp. 107–8.

[6] Although he had supported the tariff bill reported by the Ways and
Means Committee and passed by the House, McKinley together with most
of the Ohio members voted against the measure as it came from the conference, because of the lower duties it contained on wool, pig iron, and
steel rails (Olcott, Vol. I, p. 141).

Committee to tear down the protective system. He criticized the bill because of its ambiguous and complex nature. It would require, he contended, mathematical experts to calculate most of the duties. After enumerating instances to support his contention, McKinley challenged the sponsor of the Morrison bill to calculate the dutiable articles listed. "I am sure," he declared, "before they finished their work, they would pronounce this bill too complicated for human ingenuity and too uncertain for public law."[7]

No one would ever suspect, he continued, that intelligent experts like those in the tariff commission had anything to do with the Morrison bill. It bore no evidence of expert framing. It was, in fact, a piece of botched legislation. It would be far better to intrust the bill to an intelligent commission than to accept it in its present form. He denied the contention that it would benefit the farmers by opening up foreign markets for their grains. American farmers must depend on the domestic market. They could not do otherwise, since 90 per cent of the farm products raised in the United States were consumed at home. This would continue to be true as long as the population of the country was increasing at its present rate.[8]

McKinley quoted from several English publications for expressions of foreign opinion on the Morrison bill, all of which apparently approved of its provisions. He used ironic terms in speaking of the motives behind such statements by the British. "This deep solicitude of our English friends," he said, "is of course unselfish and philanthropic; it is all for our benefit, our good, our prosperity. It is disinterested purely and arises from the English manufacturers' desire to see our own grow and prosper."[9] The real interest of the British in the pending bill was their hope that it would be passed, thereby opening up this country to British manufactures. This must not be permitted. The Morrison bill must be defeated.

When the measure came up for the vote, the results showed that the protectionists were still in the saddle. Forty-one pro-

---

[7] *Speeches and Addresses*, p. 136.
[8] *Speeches and Addresses*, pp. 140–45.
[9] *Speeches and Addresses*, p. 149.

tectionist Democrats led by Randall joined the Republicans in voting it down. Yet in spite of the seeming strength of protectionism in Congress, the steady drift toward tariff reform had by this time drawn so many members of both major parties into its current that both Republicans and Democrats deemed it expedient in the Presidential campaign of 1884 to straddle the issue in their party platforms. The tariff was therefore not an issue in the contest between Blaine and Cleveland. The tariff as a political issue remained quiescent until President Cleveland delivered his celebrated message to Congress in 1887, in which, dealing solely with the tariff, he gave urgent reasons for revision of the high rates.

CHAPTER VI

The Battle Over Tariff and Surplus

Tariff reform, though seemingly strong, would doubtless have languished had it not been for the mounting surplus in the Treasury and President Cleveland's constant harping on the need of drying up the sources of the surplus by reducing tariff revenue. The presence of a surplus in the amount of $446,000,000 by 1885 had grown to be an embarrassing and disturbing problem. The surplus, it was true, had been used to pay off much of the enormous war debt. But there were limits beyond which the government could not go in the matter of debt reduction. For as the Treasury retired outstanding bonds and they appreciated in value, the government would be accused of encouraging speculation in its securities by paying bondholders premiums on their holdings. Moreover, since national banks under the national banking system were required to hold government bonds as security for their bank notes, the bonds could not be retired without undermining the national banking system. As a means of drawing on the swollen surplus the Treasury adopted the practice of distributing some of it among the national banks in exchange for their government bonds as security. In this manner, through the medium of the banks, surplus funds had got into public circulation.

In the campaign of 1884, as previously noted, neither of the major political parties made tariff revision and the surplus clear-cut party issues. In this both parties were governed by political expediency. But after Cleveland's election tariff-reform Democrats continued to push for reduction of tariff rates. In early 1886 a second Morrison bill in which a number of articles were transferred from the protected to the free list was defeated in the House. In his December message to Congress that year Cleveland termed the collection of revenue under the tariff a burdensome tax, especially on the farmers and the laboring men. But the House, though under Democratic rule, voted against considering any revenue bills. The next year, in departure from every precedent, Cleveland's whole message to Congress was devoted to the one subject of tariff reform. The raising of revenue beyond the Government's needs he denounced as extortion. Revenue so collected was money taken from the peoples' pockets and the channels of trade. The result, Cleveland declared, was a dangerous surplus in the Treasury side by side with a depleted money supply in the country. Having branded the "vicious, illegal and inequitable tariff" as responsible for these conditions, the President without question had taken sides with the tariff reformers.[1]

By 1888 the call for relief from an overflowing excess of revenue over government needs grew to be so urgent that the Secretary of the Treasury appealed to Congress for legal authority to use the surplus to redeem bonds. Although it was pointed out that he already had the authority under a previous law, the cautious Secretary insisted on more legislative support. This he was granted by resolution passed by each branch of Congress. McKinley spoke against the House resolution while it was being considered in Committee of the Whole. He held the Cleveland administration responsible for not reducing the flow of revenue into the Treasury and then failing to manage properly the resulting surplus. The Secretary of the Treasury had the power, McKinley maintained, to use the surplus to purchase outstanding bonds, but he refused to use his power. Instead, sixty million dol-

---

[1] D. R. Dewey, *National Problems,* pp. 56 ff.

lars of the surplus was farmed out to the banks to use without interest while the government must go on paying interest on bonds that might have been retired.

McKinley went so far as to accuse the Democratic administration of an ulterior motive with respect to the surplus. "I wonder," he said, "if this was not just what was in the mind of the President; I will pile up this money in the Treasury, $65,000,000 of it, and then I will tell Congress that the country will be filled with widespread disaster and financial ruin if it does not reduce the tariff duties." In imputing such motives McKinley of course did not take into account that the problem of liquidating the public debt had grown more difficult with each passing year.[2]

In response to the President's message of 1887, R. Q. Mills, chairman of the Ways and Means Committee, undertook a thoroughgoing revision of the tariff. The resulting Mills bill, as it came from the committee, had all the earmarks of a revised measure. Since one purpose was to reduce revenue, the average level of duties was sharply lowered from 47 to 40 per cent. But in this particular instance the sponsors of the bill overlooked the possibility that such a drastic lowering of rates might stimulate imports and actually result in bringing in more revenues for the surplus. The bill was also found to be unsatisfactory because it encouraged sectional discrimination along political lines. Thus iron ore mined in Southern Democratically controlled states was given protection, but the bill made heavy reduction in duties on iron and steel products made in states dominated by Republicans. The duty on Southern-grown rice was left practically unchanged, but the rate on starch manufactured in New York was cut in half. The sponsors of the Mills bill also laid themselves open to criticism because of alleged star-chamber, dark-lantern methods employed by the Ways and Means Committee. There were no public hearings, and no opportunity was given even Republican members of the committee to examine the bill before it was reported to the House.[3]

McKinley's speech on the Mills bill was perhaps characteristic

[2] *Speeches and Addresses,* pp. 269–70.
[3] Dewey, pp. 67–68.

of the kind of discussion engaged in by others who spoke against it. He used the opportunity to discuss the difference between free trade or tariff for revenue only and the protective tariff. Free trade as we had it in the United States, he said, was justified since the people as a nation had a common language, a common citizenship, and were under one flag and one constitution. Trade should therefore be free, equal, and reciprocal. But as for foreign nations, we should deny them the right to trade on equal terms with our own producers. Why should the foreigner, McKinley asked, who had no obligations of citizenship under our laws and who paid no taxes and performed no civil duties and contributed nothing to the support and progress of our nation, why should he have equal privileges of trade with American producers and taxpayers? "We put a burden upon his products," McKinley declared, "we discriminate against his merchandise because he is alien to us and our interests and we do it to protect, defend, and preserve our own who are always with us in adversity and prosperity, in sympathetic purpose and if necessary in sacrifice." That was our governing principle, said McKinley, and it was a patriotic, righteous principle. "In our country," he continued, "each citizen competes with the other in free and unresentful rivalry while with the rest of the world, all are united and together in resisting outside competition as we would foreign interference."[4]

Free foreign trade, as he conceived it, would mean inviting the products of cheap foreign labor into the American market to compete with the American product made with better, more highly paid labor. It would be like giving our money, our products, and our markets to other nations, to the loss of our tradesmen, laborers, and farmers. Protection, on the other hand, would keep money, markets, and manufactures at home for the good of our own people.

Equipped with an arsenal of statistical evidence, McKinley proceeded to assail the Mills bill and laid bare its major weaknesses. It would not, he showed, bring in less revenue, as asserted, but more. It contained glaring examples of sectional discrimina-

---

[4] *Speeches and Addresses,* pp. 294–95.

tion in favor of the Southern cotton planters and against the Western farmer. After taking the duty off the wool that the farmer raised, the bill taxed him for everything he bought. Then with mock seriousness McKinley asked what the Mills bill really did do for the farmer. He could discover only one benefit: it removed the duty from sheep-dip, a preparation of tobacco stem, sulphur, and lime used on sheep.[5]

The Mills bill was passed by a small majority. Nearly every Democratic member of the House voted for it, and all but two Republicans against it. In December, 1888, the Republican Senate framed its own tariff bill in place of the House measure and passed it by the close majority of two votes. Meanwhile the tariff had become the leading political issue of both major parties. The Republican platform of 1888, in language unmistakably clear, committed the party to the maintenance of a protective tariff. The Democrats endorsed the Mills bill, but were cautious in their position on tariff revision.

In the campaign of 1888 the Democrats were forced to defend themselves against the charge that they were for free trade. Cleveland, embarrassed by such charges, repeatedly denied that the Democratic party was for free trade. Republicans on the contrary exalted the protective tariff as an "American policy" synonymous with patriotism and calling for the loyal support of every American.

"Let England take care of herself," were McKinley's words, "let France look after her own interests, let Germany take care of her own people, but in God's name let Americans look after America."[6] Harrison's election as President and the winning of Republican majorities in both branches of Congress were naturally hailed in Republican quarters as meaning that the country itself favored protection.

McKinley's strong position in the House was made evident when the Fifty-first Congress met in December, 1889. As a candidate in the election for speaker, he was the main contender against Thomas B. Reed; he lost by a single vote. No doubt some

---

[5] *Speeches and Addresses*, p. 297.
[6] *Speeches and Addresses*, p. 257.

credit for McKinley's strength in the fight for the speakership belonged to Mark Hanna, who made a special trip to Washington to help the man whom he had decided to make his political protégé. Hanna actively canvassed the members in McKinley's behalf and secured for him several votes from Minnesota.[7]

Reed as speaker placed McKinley on the Rules Committee and made him chairman of the Ways and Means Committee. This was fitting acknowledgment that he now ranked foremost among the protectionists in Congress. Upon his shoulders and upon the majority members of Ways and Means rested the responsibility of constructing a new tariff bill.[8] In preparation for it the committee conducted extensive public hearings at which manufacturers, workingmen, and the general public could present their views. Much testimony was collected at these hearings. After nearly four months spent on the bill it was presented to the House on April 16, 1890. The new tariff bill, to be known as the McKinley bill, proposed to boost the general level of duties from 38 to nearly 50 per cent. It was a curious device designed to provide the highest protection in American tariff history along with provisions that would sharply reduce revenues. The stream of revenue that heretofore had fed the swollen Treasury surplus was to be almost dried up because of prohibitive duties contained in the bill. Moreover, by placing raw sugar on the free list the bill disposed of some fifty millions of revenue a year resulting from the former duty on imported sugar. The granting of a bounty of two cents a pound to domestic sugar growers would dip ten millions more out of the surplus, and lower excise taxes on liquor and tobacco would yield less internal revenue.

For the farmers' benefit higher duties were placed on farm products, though such products were imported in comparatively small quantities. A striking feature was the provision giving protection to certain so-called infant industries, such as the manu-

---

[7] Croly, p. 150.

[8] The Ways and Means Committee at this time numbered thirteen members. Among the eight Republicans on the committee were several besides McKinley who later became prominent for their part in tariff legislation, such as Nelson Dingley, Sereno Payne, and Robert LaFollette.

facture of tin plate and certain kinds of silk manufacture, as yet unborn infants. A final but by no means unimportant feature was the reciprocity clause added to the McKinley bill, largely at the insistence of Secretary of State Blaine. Since he was much interested in promoting American foreign trade, especially with the Latin American countries, Blaine was instrumental in securing an amendment whereby molasses, tea, coffee, and hides, products from Latin America, were to be admitted duty-free, but with a proviso that the President might place duties on these products if any nation discriminated unjustly and unreasonably against American goods.

McKinley's speech on the bill bearing his name deserves to be rated as possibly the best of his many utterances on the tariff. It showed exceptional care in the preparation and a thorough mastery of the subject, and it carried conviction to those of his hearers within earshot of the pleasing, well-modulated tones of McKinley's voice. For those demanding that the tariff be revised to insure less revenue, he could point to the prohibitive duties on many protected goods made in the United States. The bill should therefore satisfy the reformers and still not sacrifice the interest of the protectionists.[9] Then he spoke of the benefit to the farmers through increased protection by raising duties on wheat and other grains. This he thought justifiable because of growing competition from foreign agricultural products. Critics of the bill, however, called attention to the heavy exports of American grain and foodstuffs and naturally asked why protection was needed for such a healthy exporting industry as American agriculture.

As to the probable effect of the bill on the country's foreign commerce, McKinley felt confident that those were wrong who insisted that it would suffer if the bill were made law. Citing the years 1876 to 1889, when there were high protective tariffs, he showed that with the exception of two years the United States

---

[9] Figures for the first year that the McKinley tariff was in force seemed to support his contention. Receipts from customs in that year showed a decrease of about $52,000,000 (Olcott, Vol. I, p. 185).

regularly exported more than it imported.[10] McKinley, however, was not so much concerned about foreign trade. Of real importance to the nation's growth was domestic trade. The home market must be developed. "In the presence of our magnificent domestic commerce," he declared, "the commerce along our inland seas, our lakes and rivers and great railroad lines, why need we vex ourselves about foreign commerce?"[11]

A striking feature of the McKinley bill was its removal of all duties on imported raw sugar on the one hand, coupled with a bounty on raw sugar to domestic sugar growers on the other. Why, asked the chairman of Ways and Means, did the Committee propose making a law that would mean a saving of $50,000,000 in duties for foreign sugar growers and a subsidy of $10,000,000 to domestic growers? It was done because the Committee wanted the people to have free and cheap sugar, but it did not want to harm the American sugar industry. Making sugar duty-free and allowing the industry a two-cent bounty per pound of sugar produced would give American growers "complete protection against the cheaper sugar produced by the cheap labor of other countries." [12] For the Havemeyer Trust, which controlled the production of refined sugar in the United States, however, this meant that they could buy their raw sugar for a lower price than before, while a duty of one-half cent a pound on refined sugar safeguarded them from competition abroad.[13]

With the ring of sincerity in his words, the son and grandson of two generations of iron manufacturers seemed fully convinced of the benefits the country had reaped from protection. "We lead all nations in agriculture," he asserted, "we lead all nations in mining and we lead all nations in manufacturing. These are the trophies which we bring after twenty-nine years of a protective

---

[10] *Speeches and Addresses,* pp. 421–22. President Harrison's report of the foreign trade of the United States showed that in the first year the McKinley Act was in force, exports and imports increased by over $100,000,000 (Olcott, Vol. I, p. 182).

[11] *Speeches and Addresses,* p. 424.

[12] Olcott, Vol. I, p. 166.

[13] J. D. Hicks, *The American Nation,* p. 218.

tariff. Can any other system furnish such evidence of prosperity?"[14]

Passed by Congress, the McKinley bill received the President's signature on October 1. To make sure of its passage two other acts, the Sherman Anti-Trust Law and the Silver Purchase Law, were enacted as conciliatory measures, the first to satisfy those who feared the rise of tariff-fostered monopolies, the second to appease clamorous Western silver interests.

Scarcely was Harrison's signature dry when public reaction to the bill made itself felt. Congressmen whose terms were soon to expire, when they returned to their home districts to campaign for re-election, learned to their sorrow how unpopular the new McKinley tariff law was. Inasmuch as it had become law only a month before, the elections were in effect a kind of referendum on the tariff. A Congressman stumping his district was judged mainly by his record on the McKinley bill. On that record alone he was likely to stand or fall. In some cases, it is true, the gerrymander complicated the issue, but the major factor accounting for the heavy political casualties of Republican congressmen in 1890 was the malodorous tariff.

Badly handicapped in the race for re-election by another Democratic gerrymander of his district plus the odium attached to the law that bore his name, William McKinley was numbered among the many defeated ones. He was just another lame-duck congressman among many others. Was this to be the end of a promising political career? There were many who thought and hoped it would be. But time would tell. And was the verdict on the tariff given at the polls in 1890 to be final, or would it be revised? There were those who thought and hoped that the protective tariff had been relegated once and for all to the limbo of forgotten relics. But, there again, time would tell.

---

[14] *Speeches and Addresses*, p. 428.

CHAPTER VII

Darkening Skies

Farsighted observers may have noted in the elections of 1890 the ground swell of a mighty social unrest. Such in fact was the great popular revolt that was coming to a head and sweeping over the West and the South. The New South, so-called, had developed a diversified industry in the post-Civil-War period. But in spite of industrialization the South was still primarily agricultural. Most of its population depended on agriculture for a living. As in pre-Civil-War times, cotton was still the leading product, but the cotton output was almost twice as great. Other products of the South included tobacco, sugar cane, cereals, and livestock. The tendency, however, among most Southern tenant farmers was to stick to cotton-growing, partly because it was easier, and partly, too, because cotton was not perishable and could always be sold for some price.

A striking fact about Southern farmers was that 70 per cent of them were tenants, mostly Negroes and lower-class whites. Tenants who rented farms for cash or paid part of their crops as rent were mainly white and fairly prosperous. But the "share-croppers," many of them Negroes, paid most of their crops in rent to their landlords and were in a condition approaching peonage. Nearly all of them were hopelessly in debt not only to their landlords but also to country stores for goods and supplies. In time, as landlords engaged in the business of running country stores, their tenants were in debt to them both as tenants and as customers. Thus, burdened by never-ending debt, lacking in enterprise and ambition, often a victim of hookworm and pellagra, the Southern share-cropper was in desperate plight.

Southern state legislatures controlled by the Democratic Bourbon class were naturally opposed to all proposals to remedy or improve conditions of farm tenants. Their control in nearly every state in the South rested on representation so apportioned that representatives from the "black counties," where population was predominantly nonvoting Negroes, could always outvote representatives of the white counties. White supremacy was possible only by maintaining the one-party system in the South; and thus the Bourbons of the Democratic Party kept themselves in power as the favored ruling caste. That such a system would be tolerated indefinitely was unlikely. At some time there would be open revolt against it.

Parallel with the emergence of the New South was the rise of a New West, which included the region from the bend of the Missouri River to the Rocky Mountains. It took in Kansas, Nebraska, the Dakotas, parts of Colorado, Wyoming, and Montana, and the Indian Territory to the south, from which the state of Oklahoma was later formed. Unlike the New South, which was preceded by an Old or Antebellum South, the New West had come into existence since the Civil War. Most of its rapid growth was due to the railroads, which had actively promoted settlement through the sale to settlers of land given them under their land grants. Though the railroads themselves did not much profit from such land sales, they contributed tremendously to the building up of the Middle Border, the name by which this part of the West was known. Settlers moving into the region acquired land either from the railroads or in homesteads from the government and on such modest terms that the poorest could become landowners. For those who lacked the means to equip their farms

with the necessary implements, homes, and barns, abundant
credit was available from Eastern capitalists ready to lend money
secured by mortgages on the land. As a consequence, the people
in the New West differed from the people in the New South
at least in one respect: they started out not as tenants but as
owners of the land on which they settled.

Population in the New West was also more diversified than in
the South. It comprised veterans of the Civil War, farmers from
the upper Mississippi Valley, and businessmen and workingmen
from eastern states, besides many immigrants from Europe drawn
into the onsweeping stream westward to share in the prosperity of
the New West. Doubtless many who had given up the struggle
to make a living during the hard times and gone west to make a
new start bettered themselves for at least a few years. If so, how
soon they were to be disillusioned!

A succession of droughts that set in in the summer of 1887
brought despair to settlers in western Dakota, Kansas, and
Nebraska. Their crops, exposed to weeks of blazing sun and hot
winds, withered and died. The parched fields yielded a bare
pittance for man or beast. In desperation farmers abandoned
their land and started out on the dreary trek back east. Painted
on the sides of their wagons one saw the words "In God we
trusted, in Kansas we busted," or a bit of revealing verse like—

> Fifty miles to water,
> A hundred miles to wood,
> To Hell with this damned country;
> I'm going home for good.[1]

Many a settler unable to pay on his mortgage was forced off his
farm through foreclosure by a bank or loan company.

Could the western farmer whose crops were destroyed by
drought benefit from the McKinley tariff on wheat and barley?
Could the Southern farmer who sold his cotton abroad, hoping to
buy merchandise in exchange, gain from the tariff? He and the

---

[1] Hicks, *The American Nation,* p. 238 (all quotations by permission of the
Houghton Mifflin Company).

but his chief contribution was the money he collected to finance the campaign. Most of Hanna's time was devoted to securing Senator Sherman's re-election by the Ohio legislature in January, 1892. Sherman's re-election this time was made particularly uncertain by Foraker's unexpected decision to enter the contest against him for the Senatorship. The politician from Cincinnati, as was to be expected, proved to be a strong contestant, and although he lost out in the race with Sherman, its spirited nature revived the oldtime factional rivalry within the state Republican Party.[5]

The McKinley triumph so soon after his defeat and Sherman's hard-won victory over Foraker were the first real fruits Mark Hanna reaped in his career to promote his friends as candidates for public office. As for McKinley, his impressive success in returning to public life added much to his political prestige. As governor of Ohio he became a strong presidential possibility.

His first term as governor, however, was comparatively uneventful. Legislation affecting laboring men was placed on the statute books. These laws guarded against accidental injury of railway brakemen by requiring the railroads to install automatic couplers and air brakes on their cars. For the safety and comfort of streetcar motormen and conductors, street railway companies were required by law to equip their cars with safety devices and vestibules for protection against inclement and cold weather. On the governor's recommendation the Legislature enacted a law on arbitration of labor disputes based on ideas that he had advanced as Congressman. Under the law a Board of Arbitration appointed by the governor was set up, with authority to intervene in disputes involving twenty-five or more employees in the same occupation. Apparently the Board proved very effective in preventing strikes and labor disturbances through timely adjust-

---

[5] Olcott, Vol. I, pp. 271–72. The major issues in the Ohio campaign were free silver and the tariff. The election results were interpreted as a clear vindication of the Republican doctrines of sound money and protection. In a speech at Canton made after his election as governor, McKinley declared: "The American system or policy of a protective tariff has been fully vindicated and the policy of a sound and uncorrupted currency has also again signally triumphed" (*Speeches and Addresses*, p. 562).

ment of disputes. In some instances the Board was successful in settling strikes of long standing involving large numbers of workmen.[6]

The hard times that had scourged agricultural areas since the drought of 1887 reached a national scale before McKinley had long been governor. The hard times threw upon the state government of Ohio a multitude of economic and social dislocations. With these the McKinley administration struggled practically to the end of its official term.[7] The general unrest gave rise to widespread strikes, mob action, and riots. The Ohio National Guard was called into constant service by the governor to maintain order. The most serious disturbances were the coal miners' strikes occurring at Mount Sterling in April 1894 and in Guernsey County in June of that year. State troops were dispatched en masse to suppress these disorders, frequently under the governor's experienced military supervision. Public tranquillity was also disturbed by rioting and mob violence in different parts of the state, and troops were needed to quell these outbreaks. In one of them a mob seized a prisoner from the sheriff of Logan County and lynched him. In Fayette County, by the timely action of the militia, a prisoner in the county jail was rescued from the hands of an angry mob that tried to break into the courthouse in attempting to seize him.[8]

After a long period of unemployment, miners in the Hocking Valley coal fields were in destitute circumstances. The situation was brought to the governor's attention early in 1895 by representatives of the Trade Labor Union. In response to their appeal and that of the mayor of Nelsonville McKinley organized a statewide relief expedition. Through contact with the Chambers of Commerce of leading cities in the State and private charity agencies, food, clothing, and other necessities were collected and dis-

---

[6] Olcott, Vol. I, pp. 274–76. "General" J. S. Coxey's army of unemployed workmen that moved across the state in the summer of 1894 was one of several of its kind. McKinley sent militia to prevent disturbance and to preserve order.

[7] McKinley was re-elected in 1893 by a majority of more than 40,000.

[8] Jordan, pp. 308–9; Olcott, Vol. I, pp. 279–81.

tributed in sufficient quantity to feed and clothe about ten thousand persons in the stricken area.[9]

Financial aid from wealthy personal friends to rescue McKinley from bankruptcy during his second term brought upon him the charge of accepting favors from friends while a public officer.[10] Because of personal obligation to them for such favors, his critics contended that his position as governor was compromised. They chose to see in such obligation the reason for McKinley's reluctance to support legislation contrary to the interests of the corporations. The streetcar companies in which Hanna and others who befriended McKinley had interests were pointed to as examples of corporations that were not bearing their share of taxes. Yet the governor, even though the state treasury was in need of more revenue, remained indifferent to every proposal to make them pay more taxes. At the same time, it was asserted, he favored legislation to extend the franchises of these corporations.[11]

Attempts to fasten blame on McKinley for bad conditions existing in Ohio's penal and charitable institutions were also made. Many people, however, chose to take a sympathetic, understanding attitude in the matter. They realized that the governor's failings were of the mind, not of the heart, and that he was of incorruptible, irreproachable character. They knew, too, that McKinley was not responsible for many of the wrongs reported as existing in state institutions; that they were in no way connected with his administration. His partisans likewise took into account that, not having the veto, the governor's control over legislation was restricted.[12]

As a whole Governor McKinley's administration, when compared with the administrations of other chief executives of Ohio,

---

[9] Olcott, Vol. I, pp. 281–82.

[10] Having endorsed the notes of a personal friend for sums aggregating $100,000, McKinley, when unexpectedly called on by banks to meet these obligations, was faced with bankruptcy and political disaster. Prompt and substantial help in the form of gifts and loans of money from Hanna and other prominent Ohioans of means and influence enabled him to weather the crisis.

[11] H. T. Peck, *Twenty Years of the Republic, 1885–1905*, p. 468.

[12] Peck, p. 469.

seemed conservative. Certainly no one could have accused him of radicalism. Though in general his administration probably could not be credited with as much constructive legislation as those of Governors Foraker, Campbell, and Bushnell, it sponsored a number of measures of importance in addition to those previously mentioned. Laws were passed giving women limited suffrage, permitting married women to act as executors of estates, enabling married men as well as married women to sue for divorce and to obtain alimony pending divorce action, requiring midwives and physicians to report to health officers all cases of defective vision in newborn infants, prohibiting the transaction of business under false names, and requiring railroad companies to report names and addresses of stockholders.[13]

"McKinley was just a good, average governor," was the observation of a shrewd nationally known journalist. "He went along signing requisition papers, appointing state boards, making occasional speeches, wearing his gubernatorial silk hat at perfunctory ceremonies, keeping from all local issues and entanglements that might embarrass a presidential candidate. Ohio never had a more cautious governor."[14] Yet was not this to be expected of the man whom Mark Hanna earnestly hoped to promote as his candidate for the White House? Was not this, too, what one would look for in a circumspect, cautious holder of public office who was by no means unaware that he was a presidential possibility?

---

[13] Jordan, p. 310.
[14] W. A. White, *Masks in a Pageant*, p. 166 (quoted by permission of the Macmillan Company).

CHAPTER IX

Master Politician

Possessing a magnetic personality and exceptional ability as a speaker, McKinley soon drew attention to himself as a political figure. His carefully prepared and well-delivered speeches were influential factors in shaping the course of legislation in Congress. In campaigning for election McKinley could win popular support from the strongest candidates the opposite party could pit against him and in spite of obstacles thrown in his way. Three times in his career as Congressman his district was gerrymandered. The first time, in 1878, he carried it by a 1,200-vote majority, although as it had been reconstructed the district had 2,500 more Democrats than Republicans. In 1884 the district underwent more gerrymandering surgery. This time Mahoning, Columbiana, and Carroll counties were cut away and Wayne, Summit, and Medina counties were tacked on to Stark's western and northern borders; but McKinley overcame an adverse majority of nine hundred votes and won by a majority of two thousand. Two years before, when the Democrats elected thirteen of Ohio's twenty-one Congressmen, McKinley was re-elected, but by a slim majority of only eight votes. This was not because of a gerrymander, but because of a claim by the Democrats that the nomination for

Congressman in the eighteenth district should have gone to another county than Stark. As a result of a contest by his Democratic opponent in the election that year McKinley's seat was taken from him near the close of the next session.

Democratic determination to defeat McKinley finally proved successful in 1890 by means of a third gerrymander that so disfigured his district that he could not overcome a majority of three thousand adverse votes.

By this time, however, McKinley had grown to such political stature that he was one of the half dozen foremost Republican leaders in Ohio. As a result of active participation in Republican councils of the state he was a factor in his party on the national stage.[1] Since 1875 McKinley had regularly attended State Republican Conventions, usually serving on important committees like that on resolutions. In 1880 he was temporary chairman of the state convention and was named delegate-at-large to the Republican National Convention that year. As a member from Ohio of the Republican National Committee, McKinley was active in campaigning for Garfield, Republican candidate for President.[2]

McKinley's political activity naturally brought him into personal contact with other rising young politicians of Ohio. Prominent among them was J. B. Foraker of Cincinnati. Foraker, like McKinley, was a Civil War veteran and had won distinction as a soldier. After the war he read law and entered the legal profession. He soon built up a successful law business as a corporation counsel and at the age of thirty-six was a well-known member of the Cincinnati bar. Politics had a strong attraction for him, and quite early in life he won recognition as a political campaigner. Though unsuccessful at first as a candidate for public office, Foraker was elected to be one of three judges on the Superior Court of Cincinnati.[3] In 1883 Foraker became a figure in state politics when he was induced to run as a candidate for governor. At the Republican state convention that year he sought the sup-

---

[1] Olcott, Vol. I, pp. 82 ff.
[2] Olcott, Vol. I, pp. 247–49.
[3] Everett Walters, *J. B. Foraker,* p. 20.

port of several top politicians, including McKinley, and with their backing was given the nomination, though he lost the election.[4]

From this time forward McKinley's contacts with Foraker, Hanna, and other prominent Republicans of Ohio multiplied. At the Republican State Convention of 1884 all three were chosen delegates-at-large to the national convention at Chicago. As chairman of the convention McKinley, after making an adroit test of his political strength in that body, was acclaimed delegate-at-large by a rising vote amid much cheering.[5]

While Foraker and Hanna favored Senator John Sherman's nomination for President that year, McKinley felt strongly drawn toward James G. Blaine. Blaine's qualities of personal magnetism and brilliant leadership commended him to McKinley as an ideal candidate. Blaine's views on the tariff, moreover, were in accord with McKinley's.

Not long after the Republican Convention met, McKinley had an opportunity to make known his preference for Blaine over Sherman. A resolution naming J. R. Lynch as temporary chairman of the convention instead of Powell Clayton, the choice of the national committee, was proposed by Senator Lodge of Massachusetts. It was carried by the votes of the anti-Blaine delegates, whom Lodge represented. The Ohio delegation was split in two on the vote. McKinley at the head of twenty-two delegates voted for Clayton, an avowed Blaine backer, while Foraker and Hanna joined the delegates voting for the Lodge resolution.[6] The split in the Ohio delegation was made more evident when W. H. West, an Ohio delegate, made an eloquent speech nominating Blaine for President while Foraker brought forward Sherman's name as a candidate.[7]

As the balloting proceeded the outlook for Sherman grew dismal, and in order to forestall if possible Blaine's nomination

---

[4] Walters, pp. 22–25.

[5] Olcott, Vol. I, pp. 249–50.

[6] Walters, p. 27. In his account of the divided vote of the Ohio delegates on the Lodge resolution, Olcott made no mention of the stand taken by McKinley in supporting Clayton (Vol. I, pp. 252–53).

[7] Walters, p. 27.

Foraker moved to adjourn until the next day. The friends of Blaine were dismayed at the prospect of suffering a defeat at the moment when victory was in sight for their candidate. At this point, according to Olcott, McKinley openly came to their aid. In a speech on the convention floor he declared his friendship for Blaine. He summoned all of Blaine's friends to unite in calling the roll of the states for the purpose of defeating Foraker's motion. The roll was called and the motion was lost. The Convention then proceeded to the fourth ballot, which resulted in Blaine's nomination with the Ohio delegates voting unanimously for him.[8]

For not giving Sherman their united support, which he so badly needed to win the nomination, the Ohio delegates were much criticized. Sherman in bitter disappointment censured both McKinley and Foraker for their defection and for the unfortunate impression their apparently hopeless division had left on the Convention.[9] But in so doing the Ohio senator did not take into account his own shortcomings as a candidate. For Sherman distinctly lacked the qualities that would commend him to his party as a Presidential nominee with vote-getting appeal.

Political rivalry between Foraker and the McKinley-Hanna coalition was intensified by Foraker's election as governor in 1885 by a plurality of over 17,000 votes. His growing popularity in the state caused his rivals much uneasiness. When the Ohio governor made known his intention to run again for the governorship they knew that, if he were successful this time, he would be in a strong position to bid for the Presidency in 1888. To anticipate this eventuality it was decided at a secret conference at Canton in June, 1887, attended by McKinley, Hanna, and others, that they should again endorse Sherman as Ohio's choice for President in 1888, the endorsement to be made at the next Republican State Convention.[10] This, it was thought, would force Foraker to take a stand. To get Sherman's backing in his campaign for re-election as governor he must come out for Sherman

---

[8] Walters, p. 28.
[9] Walters, pp. 29–30.
[10] Walters, p. 54.

for President. Foraker's move was equally shrewd. He would not commit himself in favor of Sherman's endorsement, but indicated that he would not stand in the way if Sherman himself desired endorsement.[11]

At the Republican State Convention at Toledo Sherman was unanimously endorsed in ringing terms, and Foraker was nominated by acclamation. In the fall election of 1887 he scored another smashing victory over his Democratic opponent.

When the next state convention met in Dayton in April, 1888, Foraker was all for Sherman and pledged himself to support him for President "as long as he had a button on his coat." He was then elected delegate-at-large and chairman of the Ohio delegation to the Republican National Convention meeting in Chicago. The other delegates-at-large were McKinley, Foster, and Butterworth. On the surface, Sherman's state this time would be solidly behind him, but surface indications can often be deceiving.[12]

Although seemingly unanimous for the Ohio Senator, most of the delegates were secretly for Blaine, for whom there was much sentiment among the delegations in general. Foraker suspected his colleagues' loyalty to Sherman, and they in turn questioned whether or not he was nursing personal ambitions for the Presidency. So far as he was concerned, Foraker felt that he had reason to question the intentions of his colleagues after learning that, in the event Sherman showed weakness in the early balloting, they might go over to Blaine, or to McKinley if Hanna could induce them to switch to him. That Sherman's candidacy might after all be turned into a McKinley boom irritated the Ohio governor beyond measure and caused him to eye the situation with much suspicion.[13] When the roll of the states was called for the presentation of candidates Sherman's name was placed before the convention in a highly rhetorical speech by General Hastings of Pennsylvania. Foraker seconded the nomination in a dramatic

---

[11] Walters, p. 51.
[12] Walters, pp. 63–64.
[13] Walters, pp. 69–70.

utterance that to many who heard him sounded more as if he were starting a boom for Foraker than as if he were getting squarely behind Sherman.[14]

Up to the time balloting began and even after, Hanna seemed confident that Sherman would be nominated. But as the balloting proceeded his confidence was shaken. He had predicted that Sherman would receive a total of three hundred votes. But after going to a peak of two hundred and forty-nine the Ohio Senator's vote declined. This signaled a possible stampede for Blaine or some favorite son. But the Blaine undercurrent, though powerful in the opening days of the convention, did not broaden into a stampede. In the balloting the Ohio delegates gave undivided support to Sherman, though most of them preferred Blaine. As for Foraker, their chairman, he was tempted to join the Blaine forces if by so doing he could win for himself second place on the ticket and succeed in nipping in the bud an incipient presidential boom for McKinley.[15]

In the first three ballots McKinley received votes, two on the first two ballots and eight on the third. In a state of perplexity as to the course to pursue, he remained silent. But when on the fourth ballot a delegate from Connecticut gave him a vote, McKinley thought it time to make known that loyalty to Sherman, whom he was pledged to support, would not permit him to accept votes. He arose at once with the request that balloting stop. He addressed the convention from his seat. "I am here," he said, "as one of the chosen representatives of my state. I am here by resolution of the Republican State Convention passed without a single dissenting voice, commanding me to cast my vote for John Sherman for President and to use every endeavor for his nomination. I accepted the trust because my heart and judgment were in accord with the letter and spirit and purpose of that resolution. It has pleased certain delegates to cast their votes for me for President. I am not insensible to the honor they would do me, but in the presence of the duty resting upon me, I cannot remain silent with honor. I cannot consistently with the wish of the state

14 Walters, p. 70.
15 Walters, p. 73.

whose credentials I bear and which has trusted me, I cannot with honorable fidelity to John Sherman, who has trusted me in his cause and with his confidence, I cannot consistently with my own views of personal integrity, consent or seem to consent to permit my name to be used as a candidate before this convention. I would not respect myself if I could find it in my heart to do so or permit to be done that which could even be ground for anyone to suspect that I wavered in my loyalty to Ohio or my devotion to the chief of her choice and the chief of mine. I do not request—I demand that no delegate who would not cast reflection upon me shall cast a ballot for me."[16]

Such a candid and unqualified renunciation of the opportunity open to him did not necessarily preclude the possibility of an undercover movement in his behalf. As Sherman's chances for the nomination dwindled, McKinley's statement might even lend weight to an attempt to draft him as a candidate. During the adjournment over the weekend of June 23 a McKinley boom of considerable strength was set afoot by some of Sherman's managers. In the face of an apparent stampede for Blaine or Harrison they sent telegrams to Sherman in Washington urging him to withdraw so that McKinley's name could be brought before the convention. "Blaine will certainly be nominated," wired Murat Halstead, "unless the movement can be checked by placing McKinley in nomination and concentrating the anti-Blaine forces. Give us a word and we believe we can pull McKinley through." Hanna sent a telegram entreating Sherman to retire in favor of McKinley and thus keep out the "Blaine lunatics."[17]

The Ohio Senator would not be moved. He instructed Hanna to keep his name before the convention. He preferred defeat to retreat. He notified Foraker that he "declined the request of McKinley's friends" to withdraw. He insisted that the Ohio delegates should not break off their support until assured that Blaine would be nominated.[18] In the meantime McKinley received as-

---

[16] *Speeches and Addresses,* p. 236.

[17] Walters, p. 74 (quoted by permission of the Ohio State Archeological and Historical Society).

[18] Walters, pp. 74–75.

surance from delegates of other states that they would support him if only Sherman would step aside.[19] But they could not budge him. McKinley understood too well the principles of political give-and-take. He knew that a nomination won on such terms would at best bring only temporary triumph and might in the end cost him the election.

After Blaine's cable from Paris emphatically instructed his friends against allowing his name to go before the convention, the Ohio delegates rallied behind Foraker in a final frantic effort to secure Sherman's nomination over Harrison. At a poll of the delegates soon after receipt of Blaine's message McKinley with forty-four of his colleagues voted to support Sherman when the convention reconvened to ballot.[20] Success in this case would depend much on the votes of New York, and they were controlled by Senator Platt, who was not friendly to Sherman. On Sunday afternoon, June 24, so the story went, Senator Stephen Elkins of West Virginia, a confidant of Benjamin Harrison, invited Platt to take a carriage ride with him along Chicago's scenic Michigan Boulevard. Aside from its pleasurable aspect, that drive had seeming political implications that probably surpassed in importance many a deal or trade arranged in some smoke-filled hotel room. When the gentleman from West Virginia and the gentleman from New York returned to their hotel Elkins had Platt's word that the eighty-two votes from his state would be cast for Harrison on the morrow. The story itself came from H. L. Stoddard, editor and publisher for many years of the New York *Evening Mail*.[21]

From another source previously quoted we have a different version, to the effect that the New York delegation voted to support Sherman on the next ballot unless Harrison made a substantial gain. When balloting was resumed on Monday, June 25, through efforts of Harrison's managers his vote was raised suf-

---

19 Croly, p. 135.
20 Walters, p. 75.
21 H. L. Stoddard, *As I Knew Them*, p. 160.

ficiently to get the entire New York delegation to cast their ballots for him.[22]

Murat Halstead, editor of the Cincinnati *Commercial Gazette*, reviewing the convention proceedings, gave it as his conclusion that Sherman lost because there were too many politically ambitious contestants besides himself from his own state: McKinley, Foraker, and Harrison himself, who, though from Indiana, was born in Ohio. Basically, however, Sherman's failure in 1888, as in 1884, should have been laid to an unappealing personality and a long record in public office that, although brilliant, rendered him vulnerable to attack as a Presidential candidate. In today's slang, he simply lacked political "oomph."

A very important consequence of the Sherman defeat in 1888 was the deep personal attachment formed by Mark Hanna for McKinley. Hanna had acquired extensive business interests in Cleveland. With a natural flair for politics, he had by 1880 come to be a recognized leader in the local politics of that city. He was not interested personally in public office and apparently had no political aspirations. He had used his talents in getting good Republicans elected to municipal and county offices. Hanna's rise into national politics began in 1884, when as a delegate-at-large to the Republican National Convention he was pledged to support Sherman for President. He had much regard for the Ohio Senator as a statesman and earnestly hoped to see him elevated to the Presidency. Why not, then, work to get him into the White House? By thus associating himself with a planet of the first magnitude, Sherman's promoter might rise to become a bright luminary himself.[23]

With this possibility in mind he had worked hard for Sherman at the Chicago convention. When, to his great disappointment, the Sherman candidacy again failed, Hanna fixed his attention on McKinley, whose resolute profession of loyalty to Sherman in the face of an evident movement to secure his own nomination had deeply impressed him. Loyalty was a trait more valued by

---

[22] Walters, p. 76.
[23] Croly, pp. 130 ff.

Hanna than all others. Disloyalty was a weakness that he could not pardon. It was on that account that he had broken with Foraker, thereby terminating his friendship with the only man besides Sherman to stand in the way of Hanna's interest in McKinley. The more he studied McKinley, the more he was impressed by his adroitness as a politician and by his instinct for masking it under a cover of lofty sentiments and noble generalizations. From this time forward, Hanna came to be McKinley's political mentor, and the idea of promoting his rise in politics and making him President took definite root in Hanna's mind.[24]

---

[24] Croly, pp. 140–41.

CHAPTER X

A President in the Making

McKinley's election as governor by an impressive vote did much to strengthen him as a candidate for the Presidency. No one understood this better than Mark Hanna. He understood, too, that the time to boom him would be while he held the spotlight as governor. But should it be in the next election year? At first thought this seemed inadvisable, since President Harrison as leading Republican contender in the race could practically dictate his own re-nomination. Yet Harrison, as was well known, had made many enemies in his party who might, if they discovered any weak spots in his following, turn against him and support a candidate more to their liking. Would this not be the right moment to push for McKinley, counting on his personal popularity to win over the disaffected Harrison forces?

Though at first undecided, Hanna opened unofficial McKinley headquarters at Minneapolis. He conveyed to Foraker, delegate-at-large and chairman of the Ohio delegates to the convention, that if he would get them to back McKinley, Hanna would make amends to Foraker for his treatment of him in the past. This Foraker actually pledged himself to do, not because he liked McKinley, but because he preferred him to Harrison. At a dinner to which he invited a group of disgruntled Harrison men, Hanna frankly discussed with them in McKinley's presence his possible nomination with their support. McKinley listened to the discussion, but took no part in it. He had personally pledged himself to Harrison for renomination several months before, and he considered himself bound by that pledge.[1]

His loyalty to Harrison was put to the test soon after the convention met and he was made permanent chairman. On the first ballot forty-four of Ohio's delegates voted for McKinley and only two for Harrison.[2] McKinley then ordered the balloting to stop and demanded that a poll of the Ohio delegates be taken. He overruled the right of his alternate to vote for him and instructed him to change his vote to Harrison. But the poll when completed stood forty-three votes for McKinley to one for Harrison.[3] Next to Harrison, who received enough votes on the first ballot to be nominated, McKinley was given the largest number, a total of one hundred and eighty-two. A resolution adopted by the convention before it adjourned, conveying its thanks to McKinley for the admirable discharge of his duties as chairman, was generally accepted as a veiled suggestion that he would be the logical candidate four years hence.[4] That would be the moment for the lightning to strike.

Immediately after the convention Hanna began mapping his campaign for McKinley in 1896. A loyal McKinley partisan was made head of the Ohio Republican State Committee. Plans were made for Hanna to keep his protégé before the public by having him go on extensive speaking tours. But the unusual Democratic successes in the elections of 1892 introduced an element of uncertainty. They seemed to mean that the McKinley tariff was

---

[1] White, pp. 158–59.

[2] Walters, p. 106.

[3] Olcott, Vol. I, pp. 286–87.

[4] Olcott, Vol. I, pp. 287–88. An anecdote by H. H. Kohlsaat, an intimate of McKinley, told of the reception given him by a group of admirers when he returned to his hotel from the convention. They surrounded the carriage as it drove up, lifted him out, and carried him into the hotel, much to the embarrassment of their dignified hero. (Kohlsaat, *From McKinley to Harding*, p. 8.)

still unpopular and that, should the Cleveland administration, with a solidly Democratic Congress, succeed in passing a tariff law in keeping with the President's views, it would without a doubt complicate McKinley's prospects.

By the middle of 1893 the whole country was in the throes of a panic affecting every phase of its economy. Although this would cause the new administration much unpopularity, uncertainty as to the government's ability to maintain the gold standard, because of the drain on its gold reserve due to the Republican Silver Purchase Act of 1890 and a substantial treasury deficit instead of a surplus resulting from the Republican McKinley tariff, would be damaging to the Ohio governor's chances. To make matters worse, personal misfortune early in 1893 threatened to ruin McKinley's political future. He was suddenly called upon to make good personal notes in the amount of $100,000 which he had endorsed for a friend whom he had encouraged to go into the manufacture of tin plate. When the friend failed and the banks demanded payment, McKinley was faced with bankruptcy and a ruined career. In desperation he appealed to friends for help. Hanna stepped into the breach and personally paid much of McKinley's obligation. Then, with the assistance of some of his friends, Hanna raised enough money to cancel the entire indebtedness to the banks.[5]

---

[5] Croly, p. 170; Olcott, Vol. I, p. 288. Prominent among those who, besides Hanna, came to McKinley's assistance were M. T. Herrick, H. H. Kohlsaat, Thomas McDougal, John Hay, Charles Taft, Andrew Carnegie, C. H. Frick, and P. C. Knox. Were these men reimbursed for the sums they advanced? McKinley's biographer does not state, but he mentions that McKinley deeded his own and his wife's property to three trustees. As a means of canceling his indebtedness, McKinley proposed in a letter to Herrick that the trustees buy up the endorsed notes dollar for dollar and hold them as obligations against him to be paid off as soon as possible. "I cannot for a moment," he wrote Herrick, "entertain the suggestion of having my debts paid . . . in any other way than herein indicated, so long as I have health to earn money" (T. B. Mott, *Myron T. Herrick*, pp. 51–54; quoted by permission of Doubleday and Company). McKinley, according to this author, sent Herrick money saved from his salary as governor. The money apparently was not disbursed to the original donors but was invested by Herrick for McKinley. After McKinley's death, Herrick turned the invested fund, amounting to about $200,000, over to Mrs. McKinley. (Mott, p. 54.)

His re-election as governor by the largest majority since the
Civil War brought messages and telegrams of congratulation
from all parts of the country. The Cleveland *Leader,* after naming
him as its candidate for the Presidency, came out with a cartoon
showing Uncle Sam with his finger pointing at McKinley as the
rising sun of prosperity. The underlying suggestion conveyed by
the Cleveland paper was quickly taken over by Hanna and made
a propaganda slogan in reviving the McKinley candidacy. The
idea of associating McKinley's name and the protective tariff
with the return of prosperous times was immediately popularized,
and he was pictured and advertised to the public as the advance
agent of prosperity.[6]

The idea that McKinley's nomination and election would
restore prosperity seemed to gain ground as the hard times
dragged on; and particularly so after the Democrats in Congress
bungled their chance to reform the tariff. The Wilson Tariff of
1894 fell so far short of redeeming Democratic pledges that
Cleveland in disgust permitted it to become law unsigned. It
appeared to favor the special interests as much as the hard-hit
McKinley law. Though it was meant to be a reform tariff, there
was little of reform in the Wilson law, while as a revenue act it
failed entirely when the income-tax clause that it contained was
declared invalid by the Supreme Court. Continuing business depression, a diminishing gold reserve, and increasing government
deficits after the Wilson Tariff was in effect were convincing proof
to many that Republican claims about the injurious effects of
tariff reform on business were after all well founded. The public
was not slow to lay the blame for existing conditions at the door
of the party in power, and the election of 1894 resulted in a large
Republican majority in the lower branch of Congress.[7]

Was it not evident from this, many asked themselves, that the
protective tariff was regaining public favor, and that the people
had given the author of the McKinley act a vote of confidence?
If he were nominated, the people would elect him in the firm

---

[6] Croly, p. 171.
[7] Croly, p. 172.

belief that his election would mean the return of the tariff and business prosperity.

As he realized the popular trend, Hanna determined to push his friend's candidacy more vigorously. This, it seemed, required that Hanna himself be freed from all business management. Until now, as Croly put it, Hanna had been just a businessman and only incidentally a politician. But from this time on, in order to promote McKinley's campaign effectively, the position must be reversed. In January, 1895, he retired from the firm of Hanna & Company after having actively directed its affairs for twenty-eight years.[8] For fifteen years politics had been a pastime; now he would make politics his chief pursuit.

Hanna's first concern after retiring from business was to bring McKinley to the attention of the South by having him go and meet Republican leaders from every part of the South. During the early months of 1895 Hanna rented a house in Thomasville, Georgia, where the visitors were invited to come and enjoy a kind of house-warming. There as Hanna's guests they could meet and talk with the Governor of Ohio, the "advance agent of prosperity." White or colored, all were welcome, and few were those who failed to respond to his winning personality. Meantime Hanna, the good salesman, with a superior product on display, looked on with beaming face as he watched the Southerners being sold on McKinley. When the governor returned to Ohio, Hanna set about making the arrangements necessary to insure that there should be enough and to spare trusted Southern delegates at the next Republican National Convention. The governor, after doing well all that was expected of him, was content to let his enterprising manager carry on for him.

Similar tactics were employed later at Hanna's home in Cleveland. There Hanna had prominent Republicans from the North and West meet McKinley, apparently with very satisfactory results. Again Hanna negotiated with his guests and came to terms with them. What the terms were it would be difficult to show, but we can infer that they involved at least the giving of pledges

---

[8] Croly, pp. 173–74.

as to Federal offices to be filled in the event of Republican success. Presumably these commitments by his artful manager were acceptable to McKinley.

In the fall of 1895 Hanna got in touch with the big bosses of New York and Pennsylvania, Platt and Quay. To gain their support he was obliged to bargain on stiffer terms. Proof as to the real nature of the deals made with these powerful politicians seems to be lacking, but, as Croly stated, they doubtless involved the trading of several cabinet posts for the votes of the New York and Pennsylvania delegations. While Hanna apparently had no objections to accepting such pledges, McKinley would not be bound by promises that might compromise his integrity. "Mark, there are some things that come too high," was his reported reply to Hanna's offer. "If I were to accept the nomination on those terms, it would be worth nothing to me and less to the people."[9] McKinley's rejection of a chance to win the nomination on ethically dubious terms impressed Hanna and raised the candidate in his estimation.

Forced to admit that McKinley's position was sound and right, Hanna gave up trying to work for his nomination by cooperating with the eastern bosses. Instead, he would change the McKinley candidacy into a crusade in behalf of the people against the bosses. In order to drive home to them the righteousness of such a crusade and its irresistible success, organizations of prominent and trusted McKinley men were started in several states, notably New Jersey, Maryland, Michigan, Minnesota, and Wisconsin. In states where the politicians hoped to weaken McKinley's strength by running favorite-son candidates, methods suited to each particular situation were introduced and used with much success by Hanna and his managers.[10]

In this way delegations of doubtful states such as Indiana, Nebraska, California, and Illinois were captured by the McKinley forces. In Illinois McKinley's candidacy was personally cham-

---

[9] Olcott, Vol. 1, pp. 300–301.
[10] Croly, pp. 181–83. Favorite-son candidates were Thomas B. Reed of Maine, L. P. Martin of Indiana, Quay of Pennsylvania, Cullom of Illinois, and Allison of Iowa.

revision of it at St. Louis the week before the convention.[4] On Friday, June 12, the final revision of the plank was reported to have been made. It differed in several respects from the original draft made by McKinley, but the essential difference was in its declaration that "the existing gold standard should be preserved" until an agreement with leading countries of Europe should be made for the free and unlimited coinage of silver, to which in the meantime the Republican Party declared itself opposed.

In this form the resolution stirred up considerable discussion among those who had a hand in drafting it. One dispute arose over the authorship of the famous gold-standard plank. According to Herrick a draft made by H. C. Payne, containing the word "gold" before "standard," was submitted to the group on June 12 and adopted by it in that form. This statement was challenged by Kohlsaat, who insisted that the word was not inserted in the draft until after a long discussion and that he alone prevailed on the rest of the group to make the insertion. Herrick and Foraker both denied this. When the gold plank was completed, acceptance of it by McKinley at Canton was obtained by telegraph.[5]

In accepting the gold standard McKinley acted in full accord with the almost unanimous opinion held by businessmen and Republican leaders east of the Mississippi. To have disregarded or contravened it would have meant taking a position manifestly opposed to the prevailing sentiment of his party that there could be no real recovery from the depression until the gold standard was maintained. Although in accepting the gold-standard issue McKinley doubtless lost personal prestige because of his record on the money question, had he done otherwise it might have cost him the nomination.

In making public the gold-standard plank that they agreed on, Hanna and his advisers realized that to insure McKinley's nomi-

---

[4] The group included, besides Hanna, Senator Proctor of Vermont, M. T. Herrick, General Osborne, H. C. Payne, W. R. Merriam, M. E. Stone, and H. H. Kohlsaat. Foraker apparently was not present and had little to do in formulating the money plank (Walters, p. 130).

[5] Croly, pp. 196 ff.

nation it must have the unqualified backing of a great majority of the convention delegates. But until this could be known, they must give out the impression that an unequivocal gold standard commitment had not yet been made. For that reason Hanna, when approached by Senator Lodge of Massachusetts and others, did not show them the final draft of the currency plank as formulated on June 12 and accepted by McKinley. Whereupon Lodge pointedly warned Hanna that his state would insist on an out-and-out declaration for the gold standard and that the backers of the gold standard would at once bestir themselves and work up sentiment for it before the convention opened. So effectually was this done that when the convention convened on June 16 an irresistible sentiment for the gold standard had been built up, and its adoption was virtually certain.

Nothing could have been more gratifying to Hanna. It fitted in perfectly with his plan. He wanted to make it appear to be the overwhelming sentiment of the Republican Party as expressed in the convention that, before it would choose McKinley as its standard-bearer, he would make an unambiguous, forthright declaration for the single gold standard.[6]

The adoption of the gold standard by the Republican National Convention, however, cost it the loss of thirty-four of its delegates. Senator Teller of Colorado, who as a member of the Resolutions Committee had threatened to bolt if the convention went for the gold standard, carried the fight for the free coinage of silver into the convention. There he offered a substitute resolution, in support of which he made an earnest plea, revealing the intensely strong conviction held by free-silver Republicans. When Teller's resolution was defeated by a vote of 818 to 105, he and thirty-three other delegates from western states walked out of the convention hall.[7]

The disaffection of a comparative handful out of a total of nine hundred did not seem at all serious. Indeed, it was actually

---

[6] Croly, pp. 199–201. This is in contrast to the conclusion by Olcott that the gold plank was adopted by the Republican Party at his choice and at his direction (Olcott, Vol. I, pp. 311–12).

[7] Dewey, 320–21.

much less serious than expected. Certainly the preservation of the gold standard under McKinley's leadership had not cost the Republican party too dearly. Most delegates returned home from the convention well pleased over what had been done and confident of the results. Now that McKinley was nominated, his election would be certain.

Yet how soon they were to be disillusioned! When the Democratic National Convention met in Chicago, the free-silver faction seized control at the very outset and dictated the proceedings. This became evident from the selection of a free-silver Virginian, J. W. Daniel, as temporary chairman of the convention in place of the gold-standard Democrat D. B. Hill of New York. Over the protests of administration Democrats from eastern states, the convention did an extraordinary thing. It utterly repudiated the Cleveland administration and then adopted a platform having as its foremost plank a resolution calling for the standard silver dollar as full legal tender, coequal with gold, for the payment of all debts public and private. The Republican Party had not compromised in its stand for gold. The Democrats were determined to be equally uncompromising for silver.

As a result of Democratic tactics Republicans, instead of holding the initiative, as they had hoped and planned, were placed on the defensive. In rejecting the tariff for the currency and setting up the double instead of the single standard, the Chicago platform made a popular appeal possible. Led by the youthful silver-tongued Bryan as their standard-bearer, the Democrats could dramatize free silver as a better cure for the country's ills than the gold standard of the capitalists, the bankers, and Wall Street or the protective tariff of the industrialists. They proposed, in other words, to make the battle of the money standards into something broader and larger—a great social crusade in behalf of impoverished, debt-burdened farmers west of the Mississippi against the capitalistic, wealthy interests in the East.[8] It was also to be a sectional conflict as well as a conflict between social classes. But no matter how defined, and whether contemplated in its sectional

---

[8] Croly, pp. 204–5. This writer has an excellent account of the Republican campaign and the election of 1896.

or its social aspect, it was to be waged by the people who believed
that a sinister power was at work to take from them their due
and just share of the national wealth. This power they identified
with the moneyed interests.

Free silver, Bryan eloquently proclaimed to them, was the
cure-all of their ills. It would give the poor cheaper money in
abundant supply and enable them to pay their debts with cheaper
dollars than those they had borrowed. Cheaper dollars would
mean higher instead of lower prices for the farmer's products.
This was the message of hope and inspiration brought to them
and enthusiastically received. But it failed in its appeal to the
more prosperous farmers and wage-earners, and after the first
wave of enthusiasm was over they might be expected to show
indifference or assert opposition.

One effective way to deal with Bryan's free-silver sophistry
was to expose its fallacy to the voters, and to do this called for an
educational campaign designed to convince them that free silver
was contrary to sound economic principles; that it was a threat
not only to national economic well-being, but likewise to national
honor and integrity. In previous campaigns special efforts to
educate and win over voters in doubtful states had been made by
both major parties, little or no attention being given to states unquestionably in control of either party. But in 1896, owing to the
widespread prevalence of free-silver sentiment, obliterating state
boundaries and party lines, an intensive, systematic educational
campaign covering as much as half of the country was needed.
Responsibility for conducting such a campaign devolved mainly
on the Republican National Committee. Its role was quite like
that of a general army staff. It gave out orders to the state committees. At its head as chairman was campaign manager Hanna,
like a military strategist directing the campaign from two headquarters, one in New York and one in Chicago, ably supported
by a corps of competent managers.

In order to combat the efforts of the Democratic candidate as
he made a record-breaking tour of the country, speaking to
thousands of people and making hundreds of speeches, plans
were laid to have McKinley remain at his home in Canton, while

his audiences came there to hear him. Though most unusual, it proved in the long run to be a wise move. For the Republican candidate, had he ventured forth to compete with Bryan, would doubtless have been easily outclassed in the hurly-burly of 1896. Delegations went to Canton by railroad to see and hear McKinley as he spoke from the front porch of his home. Unlike the rough-and-tumble campaign of Bryan, these pilgrimages to Canton were carefully organized in advance. Each delegation was represented by its spokesman, who addressed McKinley in a brief speech that was edited before it was delivered. Every speech delivered by McKinley was meticulously prepared by himself and was suited to the particular group to whom it was addressed.

For the masses of the people a force of speakers was required. No efforts were spared to carry the message of the gold standard to every hamlet and crossroad. The spoken word was abundantly supplemented by great quantities of printed matter, most of it having to do with the money question. Some of this literature was printed in several foreign languages in addition to English. Extensive use was of course made of the newspapers, from great city dailies to the small country weeklies. They were supplied each week with subject matter especially prepared. The whole country was deluged with leaflets, handbills, posters, and campaign buttons.

To pay for the speakers, the tons of literature, the parades, processions, and bands, the subsidies to newspapers thought necessary to wean the people away from the sophistry of free silver, the Republican campaign chest was kept well supplied. Republican campaign managers did not suffer for want of funds, as did their opponents. Through personal contacts in New York and Chicago Hanna succeeded in collecting the sum, fabulous for that day, of $3,500,000. It set a new record for campaign funds. The contributions came chiefly from wealthy individuals and large corporations who gave liberally because they had come to identify the Republican Party with the interests of businessmen; it was the party that sponsored the two policies businessmen deemed the most essential to the nation's prosperity and progress—the protective tariff and the single gold standard. In effect

they were putting their money on the party that was campaigning to expose to the people the economic heresies proclaimed by
its Democratic opponents.

Although the campaign of 1896 was educational in the main,
it was also calculated to make an intense emotional appeal. Ex-
pedients of every sort, from torchlight processions to campaign
caps and buttons, were employed in the scramble to get votes.
Persons who remained unmoved by all that they saw and heard
or who tried to maintain a neutral position must have been rare.
No doubt many fence-sitters and silverites were frightened into
voting the Republican ticket. They may have included workingmen who were warned by their employers that if Bryan were
elected they would lose their jobs, and farmers who were told
that their mortgages would be called if the Democratic candidate
were the victor. On the other hand, the popular clamor for free
silver probably frightened many of the privileged plutocrats into
climbing aboard the McKinley bandwagon regardless of party
affiliations.

From about the middle of August, when the outlook for the
Republicans appeared dubious, the prospect of McKinley's election grew ever brighter. His victory over Bryan by a majority of
568,000, with 51 per cent of the popular vote, was impressive, for
Bryan was also the candidate of the Populists. McKinley's support came from the industrial centers of New England and the
East and from the industrial and agricultural areas of the Middle
West and the Far West. Bryan's main strength lay in the agricultural and mining region of the trans-Mississippi West. The election of 1896 signified the triumph of Republican protectionism
and monometallism over Democratic and Populist bimetallism.
It was, in short, a triumph of conservatism over radicalism.

CHAPTER XII

The McKinley Cabinet

The President-elect would naturally have his peerless campaign manager in mind for a place in his cabinet. And Mark Hanna was, in fact, McKinley's first choice for Secretary of the Treasury. When Hanna declined, the position was offered to Nelson Dingley of Maine, who after accepting resigned almost immediately because of poor health. For his third choice McKinley turned to Lyman J. Gage, a gold Democrat and banker from Chicago, who accepted the post.[1]

[1] Hanna, according to H. H. Kohlsaat, wanted to be Secretary of the Treasury, but McKinley did not think he was well qualified. When Dingley resigned it was Kohlsaat, as he told the story, who thought of Gage as an ideal candidate for the Treasury post and who persuaded Gage, who at first was not interested, to accept the position when McKinley tendered it to him. (Kohlsaat, pp. 56–58.) This does not agree with the story of Charles G. Dawes as related in his diary. According to this account Dawes and P. E. Grosscup went to Canton to urge on McKinley the appointment of Gage for the Treasury secretaryship. McKinley asked Dawes to find out Gage's views on the tariff and whether he would accept the position if it

Hanna declined the Treasury secretaryship for several reasons
He disliked the routine and confinement. Furthermore, he pre
ferred not to accept an appointment from the President, for to do
so might, he feared, leave an unfortunate impression with the
public and cause the President embarrassment. It would also
hamper his own sphere of activity. The place that Hanna par
ticularly desired, and that would give him more independence
than a cabinet position and greater freedom to exercise politica
influence, was a seat in the United States Senate as Senator from
Ohio. Hanna felt that, as Senator, he would be independent of the
executive branch and have more opportunity for self-expression
He could be more of a free lance in the Senate than in the
Cabinet.[2]

Hanna's ambition for the senatorship was eventually realized
through an understanding made soon after McKinley's election-
an understanding that involved the McKinley administration in
much unpleasant controversy, the very thing Hanna had hoped
to avoid. It resulted after several conferences between Hanna and
the President-elect. The plan, simply stated, was for the President
elect to persuade Sherman to resign his seat in the Senate and
then to appoint him Secretary of State, whereupon the Governor
of Ohio would appoint Hanna to complete Sherman's term, which
would expire in March, 1899.

Early in December, Sherman was told of the arrangement by
Hanna. After consideration he informed Hanna of his willingness
to resign from the Senate to head the State Department if the

were offered him. Two days after Dawes interviewed him, Gage informed
him that he would accept. (Dawes, *Journal*, pp. 112–13.) From H. L
Stoddard's *As I Knew Them*, pp. 245–46, we learn that Hanna had no
desire to hold office or title. He merely hoped he might reside in Washing
ton as a private citizen and as a friend and counselor of the President. But
McKinley demurred. "It would not do, you know," he was quoted as say
ing. "Everybody would be running to you either before or after seeing me
You owe it to me to come to Washington with a title to office or not at all.
At that moment the idea of inducing Sherman to resign as Senator and be
come Secretary of State had its inception. (This and other quotations by
permission of Harper and Brothers.)

[2] Croly, pp. 230–32.

appointment were offered him. An important element involved in Sherman's decision was doubtless the fact that an election of a Senator to succeed him would be held the following year, and, since the outlook for his own re-election was not reassuring, he may well have welcomed promotion to the first place in the McKinley cabinet. On January 4, 1897, McKinley tendered Sherman the office of Secretary of State, and three days later he sent his acceptance. On January 15 Sherman conferred with McKinley at Canton, and on the next day he sent his resignation from the Senate to Governor Bushnell with the request that Bushnell appoint Hanna as his successor.

By this time knowledge of what had occurred had leaked out to the press and furnished the basis of a sharp attack on Hanna and McKinley. They had entered into a bargain, it was charged, by which Sherman was to be kicked upstairs to create a vacancy for Hanna in the Senate. Sherman, it was asserted, was unfit for the State Secretaryship. The seventy-four-year-old statesman was known to be failing both physically and mentally and to be in no condition to take over the heavy duties and responsibilities of the State Department, especially when our foreign affairs were at a crisis.[3]

According to McKinley's leading biographer, there was no foundation for the charges of his critics that he appointed Sherman to be Secretary of State so that there would be a vacancy in the Senate for Hanna. The facts, declared Olcott, showed clearly that no "scheme" of that sort existed. As evidence he quoted in full a letter dated February 18 from McKinley to Hanna in which McKinley expressed regret at not being able to prevail on Hanna to accept the Postmastership or any other Cabinet place offered him. He then went on to explain that, since he could no longer put off appointing someone to be Postmaster General, he expected to offer the post to a prominent Southern Republican. There would have been no reason for this letter, Olcott concluded, if there had been a scheme to appoint Sherman to the

---

[3] Walters, pp. 133 ff.; Croly, pp. 233 ff.

Cabinet to make room for Hanna in the Senate, for the President would have known as early as January 11, when Sherman wrote him of his intention to resign, that the vacancy in the Senate intended for Hanna would follow. What reason was there, then, to try to interest Hanna in a Cabinet position?[4]

A conclusion such as this might seem probable but for the fact that we now have evidence to the contrary. While in Cleveland soon after the election, Foraker learned from Hanna himself of the plan for McKinley to appoint Sherman Secretary of State while he would be named to succeed Sherman. Hanna requested Foraker, who was close to Bushnell, to help him get his appointment from the governor. Foraker did not like the arrangement. He was not at all in favor of Sherman's elevation to the Cabinet, and he went at once to Canton to remonstrate with McKinley, but his efforts to talk the President-elect out of going through with the plan were unsuccessful.[5]

That Sherman was entirely familiar with the arrangement and a willing partner in it is made evident from his correspondence with Hanna, McKinley, and Bushnell, most of which is not included by Olcott—first, a letter in early December, 1896, in which Sherman was informed by Hanna of McKinley's decision to make him Secretary of State and of Hanna's desire to become Senator; second, Sherman's letter of December 15 advising Hanna he would accept the position if it were offered and his willingness if any opportunity presented itself to reciprocate for the assistance Hanna had given in securing his re-election in 1892;[6] third, Sherman's letter to McKinley on January 7, bearing his acceptance of the secretarial post tendered him a few days before, expressing preference for Hanna as his successor, and suggesting to McKinley that he request Governor Bushnell to appoint him;[7] fourth, Sherman's letter to Bushnell on January 16, after a conference with McKinley at Canton, containing his resignation from the

---

[4] Olcott, Vol. I, pp. 329 ff.
[5] Walters, pp. 132–33.
[6] Walters, p. 133.
[7] Walters, p. 134.

Senate and a request that the Governor appoint Hanna to the vacancy. This, he added, would be gratifying to McKinley, who attributed much of his success in the election to Hanna.[8] Meantime, in conversation with friends Sherman stated that he would not accept the secretarial post if Bushnell did not appoint Hanna.[9]

The truth of the charge that Sherman was not qualified to be Secretary of State because of physical and mental impairment was soon made obvious. The added responsibility laid on him by strained relations with Spain over Cuba proved too heavy, and the overburdened Cabinet officer failed rapidly. It became necessary to relieve him by assigning most of his duties to W. R. Day, the Assistant Secretary, who, contrary to usual practices, was invited to attend Cabinet meetings. To Sherman this was extremely humiliating. To be head of the Department in name only was a severe blow to his pride. When diplomatic relations broke down and war was declared, demands on the State Department multiplied rapidly. Sherman, realizing his inadequacy in the emergency, resigned.[10]

His keen disappointment over the incident as expressed to friends evoked much sympathy. Senator Theodore E. Burton, Sherman's biographer, declared that Sherman felt bitter toward McKinley because of having been moved from the Senate to the Cabinet so that another might have his place. In this conclusion Olcott partly concurred.[11] A strongly partisan opinion came from another author, H. T. Peck. Sherman, he declared, had no choice but to accept McKinley's offer. He gave up his seat in the Senate

---

[8] Walters, pp. 134–35.

[9] Bushnell belonged to the faction of the Republican Party of Ohio opposed to Hanna and McKinley. His preference would have been for a Bushnell or a Foraker man as Sherman's successor. He delayed Hanna's appointment until February 21 and probably acted then only under political pressure. He needed Hanna's support as a candidate for renomination for governor. He did not forward Hanna's commission until March 5, to enable Foraker to take his seat on March 4 and thus become senior Senator by one day.

[10] Olcott, Vol. I, pp. 335–36.

[11] Olcott, Vol. I, p. 336.

because he knew that he must yield to Hanna's wishes.[12] On the other hand, we are reminded by Rhodes that the Ohio Senator gladly accepted the Secretaryship because it would mean a four-year term as a high-ranking Cabinet member as compared with the two years that remained of his term in the Senate, with re-election uncertain. It was not unusual, however, for Senators to decline Cabinet appointments, Rhodes continued, and it was open to Sherman to do so; but as a matter of fact the prospect was attractive. He had enjoyed himself in the Treasury Department under Hayes, where he had had great influence with the President, and he might well have thought that a similar experience now awaited him.[13]

Authorities differ as to McKinley's failure to take sufficient stock in reports of Sherman's decline. Most of them believe that there were justifiable grounds for his action. In view of his forty years' impressive record of statesmanship, Hanna and McKinley no doubt had reason to feel confident of Sherman's ability to carry on in the Cabinet with such success as to bring much credit to the administration. Indeed, McKinley even feared, it was said, that as party leader in Ohio Sherman might seek to dominate the administration. In the circumstances, the slight importance attached to reports of his mental decay is quite understandable.

The appointment of H. A. Alger as Secretary of War has often been given as another example of mistaken judgment on McKinley's part. Judged by his previous record, which was excellent, Alger was well fitted for the office. Like McKinley, he had served as a volunteer in the Civil War with distinction and emerged as a major-general. Later he became a very successful businessman. In political life he rose to be Governor of Michigan, and in 1888

---

[12] Peck, p. 521.

[13] J. F. Rhodes, *The McKinley and Roosevelt Administrations,* pp. 32–33. Croly holds much the same view. Sherman was glad to have the Secretaryship and glad if Hanna could succeed him in the Senate. "If his retirement from the Senate was the result of a conspiracy," Croly concludes, "whereby he was kicked upstairs for Hanna's benefit, the victim himself was one of the chief conspirators" (*M. A. Hanna,* pp. 236–37; all excerpts quoted by permission of the New Republic).

he was a contender in the Republican National Convention for the Presidential nomination.[14]

The burden on the War Department because of the war demands for troops, arms, ammunition, clothing, hospital supplies, and other equipment was colossal. Under the impact the Department was almost paralyzed in its frantic efforts to recruit, equip, and train an army of sufficient size on short notice. As a general staff with military experience did not exist, blame was naturally directed at Secretary Alger. He was made the scapegoat by the public, who would have done better to hold Congress accountable for lack of foresight in not preparing for the war and for blunders by commissioned politicians in the conduct of military campaigns.

Public clamor for Alger's head grew so insistent that McKinley finally asked for his resignation. In order to quiet popular demand for an investigation of the administration's war policies the President appointed a commission which, in reporting its findings, did much to vindicate the Secretary of the charges made against him. Among other things the report referred to the general unpreparedness of the country to face the sudden war emergency. As to the provisioning of the armed forces, the report stated that the supplies were duly provided and that it would remain one of the marvels of history that the numerous demands on the industries of our people were met as promptly as they were.[15]

A story of one of McKinley's friends, if true, reveals something of his methods of choosing his Cabinet. Before making an appointment he would sound public opinion by announcing names for Cabinet positions. If the reaction to a name were favorable, he would approach the man. His first choice for Secretary of the Interior was Joseph McKenna of California, who reminded the President that, inasmuch as he was a Roman Catholic, his appointment to the Interior Department, which had charge of Indian missions, would stir up Protestant opposition. Thereupon, as the story goes, McKinley replied: "The place I want you for, Judge,

---

[14] Olcott, Vol. I, pp. 336–37.
[15] R. A. Alger, *The Spanish-American War*, p. 460.

has nothing to do with Indian missions. I want you for Attorney General." McKenna accepted at once. When J. J. McCook of West Virginia, who was McKinley's first choice for Attorney General, heard of McKenna's appointment he hurried post-haste to Canton to protest.

"I understood," he said, "I was to be Attorney General."

"Oh, no, Colonel, you are to be Secretary of the Interior," was McKinley's reply. When McCook refused the tender, McKinley selected Cornelius Bliss of New York.[16]

In making his cabinet appointments, moreover, McKinley did not necessarily choose a member of the dominant political faction of a state. Thus, in selecting C. E. Smith to succeed Gary as Post-master General, he picked a member of the anti-Quay group in Pennsylvania. To avoid an open break with the powerful Quay machine, McKinley granted Quay the right to the patronage which belonged to him as senior Senator from his state, but he permitted the new Postmaster General to distribute the appoint-ments in his department as he saw fit. It proved to be clever strategy; for by getting what he was entitled to in the matter of appointments, Quay was satisfied and at the same time the op-posing faction, more than pleased with the arrangement, was drawn more closely to the administration's support.[17]

With most of the McKinley appointments Hanna, as his coun-selor, doubtless agreed. When they disagreed, McKinley usually had his way. One instance: Hanna, it seemed, very much wanted H. C. Payne of Wisconsin to be made Postmaster General. But in the days when McKinley had been a Congressman Payne had been active in Washington as a lobbyist for the Northern Pacific Railroad. Although McKinley refused several times to consider him, Hanna persisted. But the President-elect held firmly to his decision. As reported by a well-known newspaper editor and publisher of New York, he said to Hanna, "Mark, you know I want to do anything so close to you as this seems to be, but I

[16] Kohlsaat, *From McKinley to Harding*, pp. 59–60 (this and other quo-tations by permission of Charles Scribner's Sons).

[17] J. L. Bristow, *Fraud and Politics at the Turn of the Century*, p. 60.

cannot bring into my cabinet a man who has been a lobbyist around Congress."[18]

The remaining Cabinet heads when McKinley entered the Presidency included J. A. Gary of Maryland as Postmaster General, J. D. Long of Massachusetts as Secretary of the Navy, and James Wilson of Iowa as Secretary of Agriculture. Wilson's selection was a fortunate one. He held the position for sixteen years, thereby setting a record for long service as a Cabinet member.[19] J. A. Porter of Connecticut was made Secretary to the President.[20]

A number of changes occurred during McKinley's first term, some of which have been indicated. Sherman was followed by W. R. Day as Secretary of State, and when Day went to Paris as head of the Peace Commission John Hay succeeded to the first place in the Cabinet. Alger was followed by Elihu Root as Secretary of War. J. A. Garry's successor as Postmaster General, as already mentioned, was C. E. Smith of Pennsylvania, and when Cornelius Bliss retired as Secretary of the Interior, E. A. Hitchcock of Missouri took the place. The vacancy left by Attorney General McKenna on his becoming Associate Justice of the Supreme Court was filled by J. W. Griggs of New Jersey, followed by P. C. Knox of Pennsylvania. In general, the McKinley Cabinet, as was pointed out, reflected the President's conservative temper; and only one of the members was under sixty years of age.

---

[18] Stoddard, p. 247. Stoddard for many years edited and published the New York *Evening Mail* and was long known as an outstanding journalist.

[19] Dunn, Vol. I, p. 207.

[20] Porter did not prove satisfactory, and his secretarial post devolved on George B. Cortelyou, who was the President's confidential stenographer. Porter became a kind of social secretary in the White House. (Dunn, Vol. I, pp. 208–9.)

CHAPTER XIII

Republican Prosperity

The return to power of the Republicans in 1897 has sometimes been called "an era of good feeling." Elected by a total popular vote of over 7,000,000 and a majority of 568,000, President McKinley unquestionably had the people behind him. His support came not merely from the Republicans who voted for him. He had the confidence of many who voted against him. The people in general, drawn to him by a kindly personality and handsome appearance, regarded him with feelings of good will and esteem; and the outgoing President looked upon the new Chief Executive with comparable respect and admiration. At the special invitation of Cleveland, McKinley had dinner with him on the evening before the inauguration, and on the day itself Cleveland sat beside the President-elect as their carriage moved up Pennsylvania Avenue to the Capitol and remained with him during the entire inaugural pageant. Seldom had the reins of power been handed over so graciously by one administration to the next.

To fulfill his pledge to lead the country back to prosperity, the President must have the support of Congress for the necessary legislation. Therefore, to promote cordial relations with the members on Capitol Hill, McKinley skilfully used his control of the patronage. At the outset of his administration, he established a practice by which Republican Congressmen were given the right to name all postmasters in their districts, and Senators from Republican states had the right to fill all other Federal offices, such as United States judgeships, offices of district attorneys, revenue collectors, and marshals.[1] By making these concessions McKinley knew he could generally count on having co-operation in Congress. There were exceptional cases, of course, but they were comparatively few.[2]

The handful of Republican Senators and Congressmen from the Southern states usually gave loyal support to the administration. But in order to gain support from Democratic members of the South, McKinley would sometimes go so far as to turn patronage over to them that normally would have gone to Republican Senators and Congressmen.[3]

Practical elimination from political life of a Republican Senator who dared to defy the President was illustrated in the case of G. E. Wellington of Maryland. He attempted to take McKinley to task for turning down his recommendation of a personal friend for public office. Much displeased over Wellington's defiant attitude, McKinley refused to give further consideration to his preferences for public office or to consult him about political matters in his state. Without presidential favor the Maryland Senator's prestige among his constituents withered away like a plant without moisture.[4]

McKinley's first inaugural address in effect was a blueprint of the legislative measures needed to aid business and economic recovery. Selecting as its starting point the government's need for adequate revenue, the address stressed the importance of a new protective tariff for the purpose of providing such revenue. This accomplished, the revision of the currency as the next most

---

[1] Bristow, p. 63.

[2] McKinley's skill in wielding patronage was well demonstrated in the case of Senator W. E. Chandler of New Hampshire, who at first was antagonistic to the administration but was entirely won over by McKinley's letting him have his way in naming his friend as postmaster of his home town (Bristow, pp. 64–65).

[3] See Bristow, p. 85, for the story of Senator J. L. McLaurin of South Carolina.

[4] Bristow, p. 83.

urgent need could be undertaken. For these purposes the President summoned Congress in special session on March 15.[5]

In recommending that Congress meet in special session to review the tariff, the President had the united backing of his party; and, since the Republicans controlled Congress, he could feel sure of success. Indeed, the Republican-ruled House was prepared to rush through the new tariff bill in record time. Promptly re-elected Speaker, Reed reappointed Dingley chairman of the Ways and Means Committee, most of whose members had been on the Committee in the preceding session. They had already worked on a tariff bill before the special session, and it was at once put in shape and reported to the House only four days after the session began.

By means of the "Reed Rules" the Speaker was able to push the Dingley Bill through with little debate. Only 22 of its 163 printed pages were given consideration by the House. In two weeks the bill was passed and sent to the Senate, where its progress was slowed down. As reported by the Senate's Finance Committee the Dingley Bill was a protectionist measure, but it contained duties intended only to procure revenue, and many of its protectionist rates were scaled down. It was meant to be a protective tariff, but not to an extent that would make it unpopular. Since the Senate was controlled by protectionist senators speaking for certain great corporations and manufacturers, the Dingley Bill was made over into what they believed a tariff law should be. Two months were spent on it before the protectionists in the Senate were satisfied with the bill; and when finally passed it bristled with amendments and contained many higher duties than the original House bill. Still more increases were added by the

---

[5] Olcott, Vol. I, pp. 346–49. This writer maintained that, because of a deficiency of revenue under the tariff of 1894, Cleveland was forced to borrow money to replenish the depleted gold reserve, drained to meet the government's current outlay (pp. 343–46). On the other hand, H. T. Peck contended that the $69,000,000 deficit in 1893–94 occurred under the McKinley tariff; that when McKinley called Congress into special session to restore the protective tariff the Treasury had a $9,000,000 surplus. Peck was convinced that the Wilson Act was in no way responsible for loss of revenue in 1893–95 and that, if left undisturbed, it would have yielded sufficient income for the government's current expenses (p. 523).

conference committee, with the result that the Dingley tariff, as signed by the President on July 24, had the dubious distinction of being the highest in American history.[6]

It was also one of the most complex of tariff laws, as a study of some of its provisions will show. Under the Wilson tariff raw wool was free of duty, on the supposition that, the domestic supply being insufficient to meet the demand, imports of foreign wool were needed; but the amazing growth of woolen-goods manufacture that set in caused ranch owners in the West to turn from raising cattle to raising sheep, which before long became so profitable to them that Midwestern farmers could no longer compete with the more cheaply grown product of western ranches.

The tariff makers of 1897 understood clearly that they must appease senators representing wool-growing areas in the Midwest as well as those of the wool-manufacturing interests. Having come out so strongly for the protective tariff, they must do something worth while for both groups. Above all they must act according to established party policy. Accordingly the duties put on raw wool were high enough to satisfy Midwestern sheep-raising farmers, while as a compensation to the manufacturers, who had argued strenuously against the duty on wool, a higher duty was imposed on woolen goods than any theretofore known.[7]

Duties on cotton goods were somewhat lower than those of the McKinley Act. On silk and linen goods specific instead of *ad valorem* rates were established, and more protection was given the manufacturers of those articles than under the tariff of 1890. On china and glassware the McKinley rates were restored.[8] In marked contrast with the advanced duties on many textile goods, some of them even higher than in the McKinley Act; the rates on metals in the Dingley law, particularly on iron and steel manufactures, were left as they had been in the Wilson Act. This, at first thought, would seem surprising. Always before, the manufacturers of those products had loudly clamored for more pro-

---

[6] Olcott, Vol. I, pp. 350–52.

[7] F. W. Taussig, *Tariff History of the United States*, pp. 328 ff.

[8] Taussig, pp. 335–41.

tection. Why not in 1897? Aided by the country's natural resources plus a high protective tariff, iron and steel manufacturing
had apparently by that time reached the position of a flourishing
exporting industry, able to compete not merely in the home
market but also abroad. Why, then, be concerned over more
protection when American iron and steel goods were actually
selling abroad at a profit at prices lower than in the United
States?[9]

Other rates of the Dingley Act, when compared with those of
the McKinley and Wilson tariff laws, are illuminating. During
the depression years the cost of American-made tin plate fell so
much that the high protective duties under the McKinley Act,
or even the lower Wilson duties, were more than sufficient. As a
result the Dingley law fixed the rates on tin plate at only about
two thirds of those of the McKinley schedule, and these were
accepted by the manufacturers without comment.[10]

Under the duties on sugar contained in the two previous
tariffs of 1890 and 1894 the sugar trust had materially benefited.
In 1897 the senators of the "sugar interests" were able to induce
the Senate Finance Committee to recommend a complicated
schedule of duties very favorable to the sugar refiners. But the
Senate itself rejected the schedule, restored the lower rates on raw
sugar as fixed by the House, and added a differential on the
refined product. When the bill went to conference the House
conferees held their ground against the demands of the Senate
conferees, with the result that the sugar schedule of the Dingley
Bill as adopted contained a slightly higher duty on raw sugar
and the differential on the refined product. Thus the net result,
so far as the trust was concerned, was substantially as before.[11]

In answer to arguments that the Dingley tariff rates were ex-
cessive, its sponsors pointed to the reciprocity clauses of the law.
These, they contended, would much reduce the rates. The President was given authority to make reciprocity agreements extending over two years, providing for a lowering of as much as 20

---

[9] Taussig, pp. 341 ff.
[10] Taussig, pp. 347–48.
[11] Taussig, pp. 348 ff.

per cent of the Dingley duties in return for concessions in the form of reduced duties on American products. Treaties of the second class were made with seven governments and submitted by the President to the Senate to be ratified. But that body, gripped by special interests, refused to take action.[12] In general the Dingley tariff was from 49⅞ to 52 per cent protective, the Wilson Act from 40 to 41¾ per cent so, and the McKinley Act 49½ per cent.

The important place given to the tariff was disappointing to those who thought that, since the currency question was made the overshadowing issue of the recent election campaign, it should have received first consideration by Congress. They looked to Congress to translate into law the public's desire for a single gold standard as expressed at the polls. The presence of a number of lame-duck silver Senators and Congressmen, however, would have blocked the passage of such a bill. President McKinley therefore decided to await a more opportune time to make good the Republican pledge on the gold standard. But in the meantime he secured from Congress the authority to appoint a commission to confer with representatives of other governments as to the possibility of adopting a bimetallic system by international agreement. Three commissioners, with E. O. Wolcott of Colorado as their head, learned after going abroad that the leading powers of Europe were planning to establish gold-standard currencies. Having, then, made sure that bimetallism by international understanding was impossible, the President gave undivided attention to the adoption by Congress of the single gold standard. When the opportune moment for this seemed at hand, after the election in 1898 of many new Republican Senators and Congressmen, the new administration confidently seized it to redeem its pledge under the money plank of the Republican Party platform. On March 14, 1900, the Fifty-sixth Congress passed the celebrated Gold Standard Act. By this law the content of the gold dollar

---

[12] J. H. Latané, *America as a World Power*, pp. 210–21. According to this author, the 20-per-cent reductions offered in the reciprocity treaties were not real concessions, for at the existing level the rates were about normal after making the reductions.

was set at 25.8 grains, or nine-tenths fine. The law also provided
for a gold reserve of $150,000,000 for the redemption of United
States notes, subject to the condition that they were not to be
put into circulation after their exchange for gold.[13]

Meanwhile signs of returning prosperity, apparent when the
Republicans first came into power, were by 1900 unmistakably
convincing. Having foretold that McKinley's election as the advance agent of prosperity would certainly mean the return of
better times, Republican leaders took their full share of credit
for all that was taking place. That the turn for the better was due
rather to economic forces beyond their control may not have
occurred to them. That economic recovery in time was inevitable,
regardless of political policy, was a concept not consistent with
"sound" Republican doctrines.

In the late 1890's when William McKinley became President
an upswing in the trend of prices was setting in. That this inflationary price trend was paralleled by an expansion of the
volume of money, owing to a sharp increase in the world's gold
supply, was not a coincidence. New, unexpected discoveries of
gold in Australia, South Africa, and the Klondike, together with
the development of new processes for mining and extracting it
from the ore, poured a veritable flood of new gold into a world
supply of the yellow metal that had been relatively fixed for many
years. The annual rate of gold production was almost unbeliev-
able. In the short span of seven or eight years the annual output
rose by two to two and one half times. Under our Gold Standard
Act much of this newly mined gold flowed into the channels of
our money supply. The consequences could not have been otherwise. The dollar steadily dropped in value while prices rose.
Industry and agriculture quickened in response to the inflationary
pressure on them. Soon more inflationary forces were at work: a
war with Spain and a war in South Africa, the Philippine insurrection, the Boxer Rebellion in China. Each separately and all
combined contributed to the making of a full-fledged McKinley
boom.[14]

---

[13] Olcott, Vol. I, pp. 355 ff.
[14] J. D. Hicks, *The American Nation,* pp. 247–48.

CHAPTER XIV

Heading Toward War

The President's earnest desire that Congress concentrate attention on measures designed to restore prosperity was soon chilled by urgent foreign complications. The problem of the proper policy toward the Cuban insurrection had been handed over by the outgoing administration. Cleveland had tried to keep peace by maintaining strict neutrality in the war between Spain and Cuba. He had determined not to recognize the insurgents as belligerents, and he strove to prevent filibustering expeditions from the United States from going to their aid. As a means of ending the insurrection Cleveland sought to induce Spain to grant the Cubans autonomy.

By the time McKinley was in office public sentiment in the United States had become highly inflamed against Spain. This was made clearly evident shortly after Congress met in special session.

A number of Democratic and Republican Senators were for going to war, and as a means of involving the country in war they passed a joint resolution granting recognition to the Cuban insurgents as belligerents. The resolution, because of Speaker Reed's opposition to it, was not brought before the House of Representatives.[1]

Desirous of urging the Spanish government to end hostilities in Cuba, McKinley instructed the American minister to Spain, General Woodford, to tender the friendly offices of the United States. He was to protest strongly against the inhuman, uncivilized conduct of the fighting in Cuba. The Spanish government agreed to grant autonomy under Spanish sovereignty and to conduct the war humanely if energetically. Spain's reply, though polite, expressed resentment over American interference and reminded the United States of its obligation as a neutral to stop filibustering expeditions leaving its ports for Cuba.[2]

The rather conciliatory tone of Spain's reply was due to the change of government that took place after the assassination of the Spanish prime minister. The new premier, Señor Sagasta, ordered the recall of General Weyler, whose barbarous practices in Cuba had deeply shocked the American people. He was replaced by General Blanco, and Weyler's atrocious reconcentration policy was abandoned. The Sagasta ministry promised to institute reforms. Men in prisons were to be set free, food was to be distributed, devastation to be stopped, and reparation made for property destroyed.[3]

The President's message to Congress in December, 1897 spoke encouragingly of progress made toward a peaceful solution of the Cuban problem. In words that sounded almost boastful he declared that our government had not permitted a single military expedition or armed ship to depart from our ports for

---

[1] Only fourteen Senators voted against the resolution. Among them was Hanna, who, like the President, ardently hoped to avoid war for fear of the bad effect on the course of business recovery. The Republican platform of 1896 had expressed sympathy for the Cuban people and suggested possible intervention by the United States.

[2] Olcott, Vol. II, p. 6.

[3] E. P. Oberholtzer, *A History of the United States Since the Civil War,* Vol. V, pp. 494–95.

Cuba.[4] He argued against intervention and counseled the need for patience, that the policy of the new Spanish ministry might be given a chance to prove itself.[5] Should it become our duty to intervene in Cuba because "a righteous peace" was not attainable, the necessity for such action would be "so clear as to command the support and the approval of the civilized world." [6]

On the day before Christmas, 1897, the President appealed to the nation to contribute money for the relief of destitute and starving Cubans. A Cuban Relief Committee was formed, and t, in co-operation with the Red Cross, supervised the collection of funds to be sent to the suffering. Thus the closing days of the year were gladdened with hope and cheer for the future. But the new year soon brought disappointment. The offer of home rule or autonomy by the Sagasta ministry was spurned by the insurgents and denounced by the Cuban loyalists. Bands of rebels who refused to lay down their arms laid waste the country, leaving a trail of destruction and death behind them. Inspired by a faction in Spain who opposed the government's liberal offer, Spanish loyalists in Cuba were determined to fight on until the rebels were subjugated. Riots broke out in Havana in which the rioters directed their venom against President McKinley and the United States.[7]

Day by day the failure of autonomy grew more evident, and

---

[4] American neutrality as pursued by the McKinley administration during the Cuban insurrection has been a subject of controversy. Part of it relates to the effectiveness of our efforts to stop the fitting-out of filibustering expeditions in American ports and their departure for Cuba. According to Oberholtzer, the President's statement to Congress as to our success in achieving these ends was made "with chauvinistic fervor not in full accord with the facts" (Vol. V, pp. 495–96; all quotations by permission of Mrs. Ellis P. Oberholtzer). Latané, on the other hand, states that of the expeditions illegally fitted out in the United States the great majority were stopped at the ports or intercepted after leaving port. Some managed to reach Cuba, but they were surprisingly few. Latané states, considering the long Cuban coast line to be guarded and Spain's inadequate patrolling of Cuban waters. (*America as a World Power*, p. 8.)

[5] Richardson, *Letters and Papers of the Presidents*, Vol. XIII, p. 6258.
[6] Richardson, Vol. XIII, p. 6262.
[7] Oberholtzer, pp. 499–500.

after the riots in Havana the American consul-general, Fitzhugh Lee, seemed convinced of its hopelessness. Senator Redfield Procter of Vermont, returning from a visit to Cuba, gave an eye-witness account of conditions in a speech in Congress. He reported on the pitiful plight of some 400,000 peasants in the western provinces of the island, driven into fortified towns and huddled in reconcentration camps. Outside of Havana there were only desolation, distrust, misery, and starvation. What most impressed the Vermont Senator was the spectacle of the entire population of Cuba locked in a struggle to be free of the worst misrule known.[8]

For several weeks all prospect of success for the President's policy of a peaceful solution in Cuba had disappeared. Our relations with Spain, thanks to the course of events, had taken a dismal turn for the worse. On the strength of a report to the President by the consul-general, in which he probably overstated the seriousness of the Havana riots, it was decided at Washington to send the battleship *Maine* to Cuba for the protection of American residents. The consul-general, informed only two days ahead that the *Maine* was due, advised that the battleship's visit be delayed several days to permit excitement in the Cuban capital to subside. But the *Maine*, having already sailed, reached Havana on January 25. In the light of what happened soon after, its prompt arrival was most unfortunate. The *Maine's* visit was represented to the Spanish government as an act of courtesy, and though Spain professed to regard it as a token of friendship between the two governments, it was actually displeasing to Spanish loyalists in Cuba and was freely criticized by De Lome, the Spanish minister in Washington.[9]

---

[8] Rhodes, pp. 52–53; Latané, pp. 14–15. Concerning Procter's visit to Cuba Oberholtzer makes the following comment: "While his visit was brief and his information was of little value, his sensational utterances had a wide influence" (p. 504).

[9] Latané, pp. 15–16. When the crew and even Captain Sigsbee went ashore, they were reviled and sneered at on the streets of Havana. For their own safety the crew found it necessary to go ashore as a body (Oberholtzer, Vol. V, p. 501).

On February 9 the New York *Journal,* a Hearst paper, published the translation of a letter written by De Lome to a journalist in Havana. It was addressed confidentially to a personal friend whom the Spanish minister believed he could trust. But the letter was mysteriously intercepted while in transit, evidently by agents of Cuban insurgents, and turned over to the New York paper for publication. Its contents were such as to inflame public sentiment because of the offensive references to President McKinley, whom the writer described as a weak-kneed politician bent on catering to the crowd and keeping on good terms with the jingoes of his party. When confronted with the evidence of his indiscretion, De Lome resigned and, upon the request of the State Department, was recalled by his government.[10]

On the heels of the De Lome incident came more startling news to raise the pitch of excitement. In glaring headlines the newspapers reported the destruction of the *Maine* by an explosion that cost the lives of 266 sailors and wounded over 60 more. The catastrophe occurred on the night of February 15 as the battleship lay peacefully anchored in Havana Harbor. The captain of the ill-fated ship urged the public to withhold judgment until the matter had been investigated. A naval court of inquiry appointed by the President and headed by Captain W. E. Sampson reported after an investigation lasting three weeks that the initial explosion was caused by submarine mines. The Spanish government conducted an independent investigation and announced as the result of its findings that the *Maine*'s destruction was caused by an internal explosion. The American court of inquiry, in making its report, did not attempt to fix responsibility for the disaster. But the tendency of the Americans was to be hasty in their conclusion that the Spaniards were responsible, though it did not seem reasonable that the Spanish government would be guilty of such a crime while its ministers were trying to maintain cordial relations with the United States. It seemed more logical to infer that the explosion had been the

---

[10] Latané, pp. 16–17; Oberholtzer, Vol. V, pp. 500–501.

work of Cuban insurgents or their sympathizers, for the purpose of drawing Spain and the United States into war.[11]

Most Americans, however, after reading the naval court's report, joined in the war clamor of the yellow press. Only a few newspapers cautioned their readers not to be swept off their feet by the gusts of an overpowering war spirit, evidence of which was everywhere to be seen. Flags were unfurled; signs bearing the slogan "Remember the *Maine*" appeared on all sides. Not since the days of 1861 had there been such an upsurge of hysteria. In Spain it was the same. Public opinion was at a high pitch against the United States. Had a poll been taken, it would have shown that both countries were ready for war. The tremendous pull in that direction made it difficult for their governments to remain at peace.

In the United States the war party comprised most of the people. Its spokesmen were the leading newspapers and eminent public men in Congress and outside. Opposed were the President, the Vice-President, the Speaker, most of the Cabinet, and a number of senators, among them Hanna. Their support came mainly from the intellectual class, the sugar planters, and the business and financial elements. All the while the President resolutely and patiently negotiated for a peaceful settlement of the Cuban problem. But the riots in Havana convinced him of the futility of autonomy. The Spanish ministry, on the other hand, still hoped for a policy of autonomy for Cuba before the United States should come out with a demand that the war be ended by granting the Cubans complete independence.

On March 29 General Woodford presented to the Spanish ministry an ultimatum from the United States. Its terms called for an immediate cessation of hostilities and an armistice until October 1, during which Spain and Cuba, with the friendly aid of the President, were to negotiate a peace treaty granting to

---

[11] Latané, pp. 18–19. The report of the American naval board in 1898 was substantiated in 1911, when a board of Army and Navy officers examined the exposed wreck of the *Maine* as it lay in the harbor. They reported that the explosion that destroyed the warship was external and was followed by a series of explosions in the reserve and forward magazines where powder was stored (Rhodes, pp. 50–51).

Cuba full self-government or independence, the very thing the ministry had been hoping to escape.[12] Two days later the American minister received Spain's reply offering certain counterproposals, but evading the demand for an armistice. Still hopeful, Woodford appealed to his government to defer action. But again, as before, Spain persisted in her policy of temporizing, and dispatches received from Madrid made no offer of an armistice.[13]

By this time Congress had become a seething caldron of war passion. The war party was now clamoring that the President lay before Congress at the earliest moment all the facts concerning his negotiations with Spain. They demanded an assurance that, if negotiations for an immediate peace in Cuba broke down, the President would so instruct Congress. He was advised by friends in Congress of their fears that some immediate action might follow unless he complied. A resolution for intervention by the United States in behalf of the Cuban insurgents might be rushed through both Houses in spite of anything they could do to the contrary. A declaration of war over the President's head would put him in the humiliating position of a commander-in-chief forced to direct the armed forces in a war not of his own choice.[14]

While the war passion was at a white heat over the report of the naval board concerning the *Maine* disaster, Senator Foraker, an ardent interventionist, introduced resolutions calling for the independence of Cuba, condemning Spain's war as "cruel, barbarous and inhuman," and demanding therefore that Spain withdraw her land and naval forces from the island. The President was empowered to use the armed forces, if necessary, to make these resolutions effective. They were referred to the Committee on Foreign Relations, while Congress waited impatiently to hear from the President.[15] He was under great pressure from Senators,

---

[12] Olcott, Vol. II, pp. 19–22; Latané, pp. 19–20.

[13] Olcott, Vol. II, pp. 22–24; Latané, pp. 21–22.

[14] When a bill appropriating $50,000,000 to be used at the President's discretion for national defense was introduced, the leading non-interventionists in the Senate, Aldrich, Hanna, Allison, O. H. Platt, Hale, Spooner, and Fairbanks, were unable to block its passage (Walters, p. 148).

[15] Walters, pp. 149–50.

Representatives, and other interventionists who tried to force
him to come out for war. "Doesn't your President know where
the war-declaring power is lodged? Tell him if he doesn't do
something, Congress will exercise the power." These were the
threatening words of a belligerent Senator to the Assistant Secretary of State.[16]

A Congressman opposed to intervention told of a committee
of Republican Congressmen who went to the White House and
informed the President that they, with the help of the Democrats,
would put through a declaration of war if he did not send a
message to Congress recommending war.[17]

The Secretary of War urged a Senator to advise the President
to recommend war. "He is making a great mistake," he told the
Senator. "He is in danger of ruining himself and the Republican
Party by standing in the way of the people's wishes. Congress
will declare war in spite of him. He'll get run over and the party
with him." [18] The Senator did not agree. The President, he declared, knew what he was doing. His advice to the Secretary
was to stand by him.[19]

Party considerations weighed heavily on the minds of the
interventionists. Senator Lodge of Massachusetts was one who
feared that, if McKinley did not declare for Cuban independence,
the Republican Party would go down to defeat. He would have
thought it hardly less odious to have brought free silver to the
country by sacrificing the Republican Party.[20] Senator Foraker
wrote Governor Bushnell that he had seen the President and
urged him to decide for intervention and independence; that the
President would favor intervention, but not independence.[21]
On a hectic morning in early April, according to Olcott, the
President, surrounded by a roomful of Senators and Congressmen, sat at his desk, on which lay his war message still unsigned.
They besought him by every known means of pressure to sign

16 Olcott, Vol. II, p. 28.
17 Rhodes, p. 60.
18 Olcott, Vol. II, p. 28.
19 Oberholtzer, Vol. V, p. 504.
20 Oberholtzer, Vol. V, p. 504.
21 Walters, p. 150.

the message and send it to Congress. If he put it off another day, he was told, his reputation would be ruined. At the time he was awaiting further word from Woodford at Madrid regarding Spain's reply as to an armistice. He was also waiting to hear from American Consul-General Lee whether Americans in Cuba would be in peril if war were declared before they could leave. Some of those present, not willing to trust the President, continued to clamor for action. Then came a cablegram from Lee stating that many Americans were still in danger. At this point, as Olcott put it, the President, pale and haggard, pounded the desk with his fist, got up, and said: "That message shall not go to Congress as long as there is a single American life in danger in Cuba." He turned to instruct his secretary to put it into the safe until called for.[22]

Besides Congressmen, the President's callers during this critical time included personages of high eminence. Archbishop Ireland of St. Paul came to the White House to present an appeal for peace from the Pope. On April 6 a delegation of representatives from Great Britain, France, Germany, Austro-Hungary, Russia, and Italy presented a joint note addressed to the President and the American people. It was an appeal to "their feelings of humanity and moderation" and expressed hope that negotiations would continue until an agreement that would bring peace and restore order in Cuba should be concluded. In reply the President, speaking for the United States, made known his gratitude to the Powers for the "humanitarian and disinterested character" of their appeal. He had confidence that they would appreciate the unselfishness of the American people in doing their duty to humanity by ending a condition that had grown to be intolerable.[23]

In making their formal appeal the Powers hoped, of course, that the American Chief Executive would persist in negotiating for a peace settlement with Spain. But the futility of further negotiations had been brought home to him only two days before

---

[22] Olcott, Vol. II, pp. 28–29; Stoddard, p. 230.
[23] Olcott, Vol. II, pp. 24 ff.

when he learned from the Spanish minister that his government, in renewing its proposal of autonomy to induce the Cubans to lay down their arms, had no intention of complying with his ultimatum as to an armistice. Convinced that his demand had been ignored, McKinley decided not to delay. He would send in his war message on April 6 and let Congress take over the responsibility.[24]

But on April 6 he withheld the message until the following Monday because of a telegram from Lee asking for more time to get the Americans safely out of Havana. On April 9 the Powers appealed to the Spanish ministry to accede to the Pope's entreaty to grant an armistice. The next day the State Department was informed by the Spanish minister that the Queen of Spain had ordered General Blanco to suspend hostilities, and that when the Cuban Parliament met on May 4 the Cubans would have all the liberty they could reasonably expect. Since this did not fully satisfy the terms imposed by our government, the President decided merely to include this latest communication in the message to be sent to Congress on the following day.[25]

In the message the President reviewed the course of negotiations with Spain to justify his contention that every expedient to end the intolerable situation in Cuba had been exhausted. The issue was now with Congress. "In the name of humanity, in the name of civilization, in behalf of endangered American interests which give us the right and duty to speak and act," he asserted, "the war in Cuba must stop." To accomplish these ends he asked Congress for authority to use the naval and military forces of the United States.[26]

Now that the matter was in the hands of Congress, the hard-pressed Chief Executive must have welcomed a brief respite

---

[24] Latané, pp. 22–23.

[25] Latané, pp. 23–24. The same day, April 10, Woodford telegraphed the President that, if given full authority by Congress, he might get a settlement before August 1 on the basis of autonomy, independence, or cession of Cuba to the United States. The Spanish government, he believed, was moving toward a settlement as fast as could be expected.

[26] Richardson, Vol. XIII, p. 6292.

from the ordeal he had undergone. Naturally averse to war, McKinley suffered severely while laboring to stem the irresistible war current. It was not the money that it would cost or the property destroyed by the war, he told Senator Fairbanks, that concerned him so much as the thought of the suffering it would bring into thousands of homes in the country. He dreaded, too, the unforeseeable problems that would surely come up after the war.[27] And he feared the effects on the Republican Party. It might be split asunder. Was the nation really prepared for war? A friend quoted from a conversation with the President at the White House. "I have been through a trying period," he said. "Mrs. McKinley has been in poorer health than usual. It seems to me I have not slept over three hours a night for two weeks. Congress is trying to drive us into war with Spain. The Spanish fleet is in Cuban waters and we haven't enough ammunition on the Atlantic seacoast to fire a salute." [28]

McKinley has been much criticized for yielding to the popular clamor for war. His critics pointed to the last communication received from Spain as evidence that the Spaniards did comply with the President's terms. To this conclusion some writers, like Latané, have taken exception. The details and duration of the suspension of hostilities, they declare, were not made definite, but were left to the discretion of General Blanco. The promise that the Cubans would have as much liberty as they could wish for was very vague. It certainly was not a guarantee of independence.[29]

Had McKinley held to his original policy of negotiating for a peaceful solution of the Cuban problem, "he might well have ruined his administration and split his party without actually preserving peace," was the opinion given by Hanna's biographer. "Congress wanted war and had the power to declare it. The people were willing. If war had been declared in spite of his opposition, neither Congress nor the country would have had sufficient

---

[27] Stoddard, p. 252.
[28] Kohlsaat, p. 67.
[29] Latané, pp. 24–25.

confidence in him as the commander-in-chief of its army and navy." [30]

Most of his critics, however, blamed McKinley for giving in to the war party. If he had held courageously to his original insistence on peace, he might have avoided hostilities, and the country would have been spared an unnecessary war. But he so much feared a rupture in the Republican Party, was the conclusion of the historian Rhodes, that he could not muster up the courage to resist.[31] He gave in to the war party although Spain was ready to meet most of his demands, was the judgment of another author.[32] By others it was pointed out that, given more time, Spain would have satisfied the demands of the United States in full. Woodford, who so well understood the temper of the Spanish government, appealed frantically to the President for more time, and had it been granted he could have gained the peace he had tried so hard for. Still another writer concluded that McKinley deserved neither praise nor blame. According to his contention, war between the United States and Spain had been inevitable ever since the Cubans revolted against Spain in 1868. That war came when it did, thirty years later, was merely the result of pure chance.[33]

No doubt there was much truth in the comment made later by the President himself when he said that "if he had been left alone, he could have concluded an arrangement with the Spanish under which the Spanish troops would have been withdrawn from Cuba without a war." [34]

On April 13 the chairman of the Senate Foreign Relations Committee reported to the Senate a set of resolutions that in general resembled those introduced by Foraker two weeks before. The main difference was that one of the resolutions

---

[30] Croly, p. 278.

[31] Rhodes, p. 64. This author was certain that if Hanna had been President we should have had no war.

[32] Walters, p. 150.

[33] Peck, p. 664.

[34] Hicks, p. 312. This author's conclusion is that war did not result from a breakdown of diplomacy, as often supposed. War resulted, although diplomacy was entirely successful (p. 313).

granted recognition to the Cuban insurgents' government. It had been included after four members of the committee presented a minority report favoring recognition. The Senate also added an amendment offered by Senator Teller disclaiming any intention on the part of the United States to exercise sovereign control over Cuba. Except for these two amendments, the resolutions adopted by the House and Senate were alike.

The amendment by Senator Teller became the subject of a heated debate that lasted two days. In order to reach an agreement between the Senate and the House a joint conference committee was appointed. After laboring far into the night of April 18 the conferees at length succeeded in their purpose. Meantime a group of Congressmen, while waiting in the House lobby for the conference committee report, contributed something to the impressiveness and color of the occasion as they sang "The Battle Hymn of the Republic" and "Hang General Weyler to a Sour Apple Tree." As day dawned on April 19, after the Senate conferees had yielded ground, the joint committee reported in favor of dropping the amendment granting recognition to Cuba and retaining the Teller resolution. The report of the conferees was approved by both houses, and the resolutions were sent to the White House and signed by the President on April 20.[35]

---

[35] Latané, pp. 25–27; Walters, pp. 150–51.

CHAPTER XV

The War President

The United States entered the war with Spain, as it had entered every previous war, totally unprepared. No one understood this unreadiness better than the President. Even while negotiating with Spain in the hope of averting hostilities he had given anxious thought to the country's alarming unpreparedness for war if his peace policy should fail. He must in some way prepare for war without seeming to encourage it. As a step in that direction the President summoned Joseph G. Cannon, Chairman of the House Ways and Means Committee, to the White House for conference. It was early in March and more than a month before sending his message recommending war to Congress. When Cannon arrived in the library the President was in an agitated state; he paced the floor nervously as he explained the situation. He was doing everything possible, he told Cannon, to prevent war, but if it came the country must be ready. Congress must appropriate money at once for such a contingency. "Who knows," he asked, "where this war will lead us? it may be more than a war with Spain." [1]

---

[1] Walter Millis, *The Martial Spirit*, pp. 115–16 (all quotations by permission of the Houghton Mifflin Company).

Cannon suggested that the President draft a message to Congress asking for an appropriation, but that he did not want to do while he was still negotiating for peace. That, McKinley thought, would seem too much like an act of duplicity and double-dealing. Would it not be possible for Cannon's committee to introduce a bill for an appropriation? When Cannon consented to have this done if the President would draw up the bill, McKinley picked up a telegraph blank from the table, wrote on it the words: "For national defense, fifty million dollars," and handed it to him.

That evening Cannon prepared the bill at his hotel. The next day it was reported in the House. Three days later it was passed by a unanimous vote and then rushed through the Senate without a dissenting vote. Never in his experience as a Congressman had Cannon witnessed such unanimity in lawmaking by Congress. Nor was it probable that he would ever again witness anything like it in his long term as Speaker of the House.[2] Of the $50,000,000, $16,000,000 was allotted to the Army, practically all to be spent on coastal fortifications, and $30,000,000 went to the Navy for the purchase of merchantmen to be converted into auxiliary cruisers if war came.[3]

Strangely enough, the first belligerent act came not from Congress but from the President himself before Congress had even declared war. On April 22, three days before the declaration, he proclaimed a naval blockade of the northern coast of Cuba. When Congress declared war on April 25 it stipulated that a state of war had existed since April 22, the day on which the President had ordered the blockade. In this way Congress was careful to avoid the impression that our entry into war was an act of aggression.

From the first confusion that attended the declaration of war there emerged in tentative form the administration program for waging it. Under a law hurriedly put through Congress the President issued a call for 125,000 volunteers, followed shortly by a second call for 75,000 more. The enlisted men were to be

[2] Millis, pp. 116–17.
[3] Millis, p. 118.

sent to various training camps. At the same time the regular
army was raised from 28,000 to 61,000 officers and men, to be
concentrated at Chickamauga Park in Tennessee, and at Tampa.

These measures had been recommended by Major General
Miles, who was in command of the Army; they were part of a
military campaign mapped out by him for a direct attack on
Cuba. The attack, however, was not to be made until fall, the
troops to be kept meantime in healthful training camps in the
United States during the dangerous tropical summer months
when yellow fever and other deadly diseases were prevalent in
Cuba. In furtherance of this plan Miles recommended that the
task of driving the Spaniards out of Cuba be left to Cuban
insurgents accustomed to fighting in the tropics. Should they
succeed with the help of the American Navy, our troops could
then be sent as an army of occupation.

But the Miles plan was soon found to be impracticable. For
one thing the Cuban insurgents generally proved to be of poor
fighting stuff compared with the Spanish veterans, and small
dependence could be placed in them. Nor would the flaming
war-spirited Americans be content to remain quietly at home
and inactive. Volunteers everywhere were flocking to recruiting
stations to enlist. The capital was alive with patriots who came
to lay their military talents on their country's altar. All over the
nation, people thrilled to the words of enthusiastic speakers
about sending armed forces to invade Cuba. America was itch-
ing to get into the long-awaited war. The President, his ear close
to the popular pulse, deemed a revision of military strategy in
the Cuban theater to be expedient.[4]

The first actual fighting did not take place in Cuba, where
Congress had authorized armed intervention, but on the other
side of the globe in the Philippine Islands, of whose existence the
American people at the time had only the vaguest conception.
This order of events was largely the doing of the aggressive
young Assistant Secretary of the Navy, Theodore Roosevelt.
Roosevelt had been appointed to the Navy Department by the

---

[4] Millis, pp. 174–75.

President at the instigation of his friends and some of McKinley's friends, among whom incidentally were several who had helped to pay McKinley's debts some years earlier.[5] No sooner had Roosevelt been appointed than he practically took charge of the department's affairs.

Shortly after the *Maine* disaster, in the absence of his chief and without his consent, Roosevelt sent secret instructions to Commander George Dewey in Hong Kong, China, to be ready to proceed with his squadron to the Philippines and attack the Spanish fleet in Manila Bay the moment war was declared. In compliance with these instructions Dewey made ready for the attack. The President first learned of this order just a few days before war was declared, and he apparently gave his approval to the instructions sent Dewey following the declaration. On that fateful 27th day of April, 1898, when Dewey's ships sailed from Hong Kong for Manila Bay, they were bound on a mission not at all contemplated in the resolutions of Congress for intervention in Cuba by the armed forces of the United States, though it was a mission to be fraught with consequences unanticipated and momentous.

On the evening of May 1 fragmentary dispatches reached Washington by cable from Madrid of a naval battle on that day in Manila Bay. First reports were vague and confusing. But as more information came in the crowds gathering to read the bulletins concluded that Dewey had won a smashing victory and hailed him as the war's first hero and next President. Next morning the papers were full of news about the total destruction of the Spanish fleet. Curiously, no word had come from Dewey himself. In fact there was no word from him until May 7, six days after the battle. By that time, however, the President in conference with his Secretaries of the Navy and Army and Major-General Miles, had made some weighty decisions about

---

[5] H. F. Pringle, *Theodore Roosevelt*, pp. 165–66. Soon after his appointment to the Navy Roosevelt openly vented his scorn for McKinley's Cuban peace policy and even voiced contempt for the President himself, whom he spoke of as a "white-livered cur" and as having "no more backbone than a chocolate eclair" (Oberholtzer, Vol. V, p. 518).

the war.[6] First, it was thought necessary that a large army of regular and volunteer troops be sent to Cuba. Only a week before, the President had assured the public "that no matter what clamor the newspapers made, he would not order the volunteers into Cuba during the sickly season. He would wait until autumn." [7] Would it matter so much, though, if they were sent there sooner? After all, the people were only too eager to get on with the war in Cuba and win it.[8]

What seemed more surprising was the President's decision on May 2, five days before getting official word of Dewey's victory, to have American troops mobilized and shipped over to the Philippines. Presumably they were to be sent to aid the Filipinos in their struggle to liberate themselves from Spanish rule. Should this aid result in the conquest of the Philippines by American arms, there was no Teller Amendment to prevent military occupation and possession of the islands by the United States.[9]

And now events were occurring in and about Cuba that seemed to make an immediate invasion of the island all the more urgent. On May 29 Admiral Cervera's fleet was discovered in Santiago Harbor by the American Naval commanders Sampson and Schley after weeks of speculation as to its whereabouts. The handful of under-par cruisers and partly useless destroyers had been in hiding there for ten days after limping across the Atlantic and completely eluding their pursuers, who had been cruising around the Caribbean in search of them. Having finally tracked down the enemy's ships after the game of hide-and-seek, Sampson and Schley proceeded to seal them up in Santiago Harbor by means of a naval blockade.[10] The President and the

---

[6] Millis, pp. 171 ff. The first official report received at Washington on May 7 was brought from Manila to Hong Kong by the revenue cutter *McCullough.* From Hong Kong it was cabled to Washington. (George Dewey, *Autobiography,* pp. 237–38.)

[7] Millis, p. 166.

[8] Millis, pp. 173–74.

[9] For an interesting and suggestive discussion of the question whether American military conquest and occupation of the Philippines was prompted by a desire to annex them, see Millis, pp. 174–76.

[10] Oberholtzer, Vol. V, pp. 530–32.

War Department then decided that it was time for the troops
stationed at Tampa to embark for the southern coast of Cuba to
co-operate with the blockading fleet in sinking Cervera's ailing
ships and capturing the city of Santiago.

It devolved upon the three-hundred-pound General Shafter
to organize for immediate shipment to Cuba the 17,000 infantry,
cavalry, and artillery troops under his command at Tampa.
Hectic days and nights were spent collecting the necessary stores,
many of them still loaded in boxcars standing on sidings. These
cars had to be located and broken open to get at their contents.
Once this had been done the supplies were unloaded, conveyed
by wagon or on mules to the pier several miles distant, and
dumped there without order or system. In the meantime the
troops at Tampa were restless to be on the march.[11]

At length, on the morning of June 8, the orders to march were
given, and the first of the regiments reached the pier. But, lacking instructions as to the order and manner in which they were
to go aboard the transports, the troops were thrown on their own
initiative. In the wild stampede to get aboard, some regiments
displayed more than ordinary ingenuity. As might well have
been expected, when it came to coping with a situation such as
this, Lieutenant-Colonel Roosevelt and Colonel Leonard Wood,
in command of the First Volunteer Cavalry, the celebrated
Rough Riders, quickly rose to the occasion. Determined not to
be left behind in the shuffle, the enterprising colonel seized some
empty coal cars bound for the pier. At the pier Roosevelt and
Wood learned that the Rough Riders were to go on board the
transport *Yucatan.* But when Roosevelt discovered that the Sev-
enty-first New York Volunteers and the Second Regular Infantry
were also assigned to the *Yucatan* he rushed his regiment to the
pier at the double-quick in time to be the first to scramble
aboard. Four companies of army infantry managed to get on
board too, but the New York Volunteers were left behind. Their
officers were not to be outdone. By ingenious means they con-

---

[11] Millis, p. 244.

trived to get their regiment on to the *Largestand,* best of the transports.[12]

The expedition from Tampa arrived in Cuba on June 22, just as the rainy season was setting in. The troops were unseasoned for tropical life, and according to Major General Miles they were inadequately trained. In a report to the War Department Miles stated that from 30 to 40 per cent of the volunteers were undrilled, and in one regiment over three hundred men had never fired a gun.[13] In general the volunteers did not compare well with the regulars in marksmanship, steadiness, and self-control. The regular troops, however, found themselves in a region altogether different from the western treeless plains to which they were accustomed while engaged in fighting savage tribesmen. Their experience in the Indian wars was in many ways a detriment when it came to fighting in the dense, impassable jungles of Cuba.[14]

The first landing was at Daiquiri, scarcely more than a dent in the exposed coastline. Landing operations were soon shifted to Siboney, several miles to the west, which became the main base of the Fifth Army Corps. Wishing to speed the campaign against Santiago, General Shafter ordered General Lawton to guard a trail leading to Santiago while the army completed disembarkation; but Shafter's zeal to be up and at the enemy was not quite up to that of some of his staff officers, notably General

---

[12] Millis, pp. 244–48. Most authorities agree as to the unprecedented confusion that accompanied embarkation of the troops at Tampa, the overcrowded condition of the transports en route to Cuba, and the disembarkation of the troops arriving there. After reviewing at some length the conditions at Tampa when the troops were embarking, Secretary of War Alger concluded: "In the great stress of circumstances under which the expedition sailed, it was inevitable that there should be much confusion and congestion. The fact remains, however, that one week from the date of receipt of orders to prepare to sail, Shafter had his men, animals, and supplies on board the transports and despite the crowding and the week's delay caused by the report of the 'phantom fleet,' all arrived off Santiago little the worse for the voyage. . . . The expedition from Tampa was a success and unmarred by loss of life or treasure." (R. A. Alger, *The Spanish-American War,* p. 82; quoted by permission of Harper and Brothers.)

[13] Alger, p. 69.

[14] Alger, p. 69.

Joseph Wheeler, an ex-Confederate cavalry veteran and the former Assistant Secretary of the Navy, who was now to give vent to
his uninhibited energies as a lieutenant-colonel.

Eager for the chance to strike the first blow, Wheeler in the
darkness of night outflanked Lawton's infantry and led part of
his brigade of cavalrymen, including the Rough Riders, into a
skirmish with a Spanish outpost.[15] This battle of Las Guasimas,
resulting in forty-six killed and fifty wounded, was heralded as
a great victory, although by some writers its importance in the
general campaign has been questioned.[16]

A week later the advance on Santiago was begun. It involved,
first, the taking of two strategic positions, San Juan Hill and El
Caney, commanding the road to Santiago. Both posts were well
garrisoned by the Spaniards. The advance against them was
over difficult terrain, much of it densely covered with jungle and
entirely unfamiliar to the Americans. The first attack against
El Caney was led by General Lawton in the early morning of
July 1, but the strongly defended position was not taken until
late afternoon. By that time an assault on San Juan Hill was
under way. As marksmen the Americans were superior to the
enemy, but the Spaniards had a decided advantage in the use
of smokeless powder. In advancing on San Juan Hill the Americans could move but slowly along the narrow, uneven wagon
road, and they were exposed the while to the enemy's long-range
firing. Not until they came within close range of the rifle pits
outside San Juan ridge could the American troops return the fire.

When, finally, they could get into formation an uneven line
of blue-shirted soldiers led by their officers, but often on their
own, charged across a stretch of comparatively open terrain and
in the face of galling rifle fire reached the crest of the ridge and
dropped into the abandoned enemy trenches. Fighting went on
for two more days, but the situation for the Americans remained
unchanged. The Spaniards fell back toward Santiago.

News of the victory at San Juan reached the President and

---

[15] F. E. Chadwick, *Relations of the United States and Spain,* Vol. II, pp.
12, 62.

[16] Millis, pp. 271–76; Oberholtzer, Vol. V, p. 536.

his advisers at Washington on July 3. But they were dismayed to learn from Shafter's message of his intention to order the troops to retire from the position they held instead of preparing to advance upon Santiago. The American troops, Shafter informed them, had suffered heavy casualties, and there were many sick and wounded in his army. That long, hot July day, perhaps the darkest of the war, the President and his Army and Navy Secretaries spent studying pinpricked war maps while they sat waiting hour after hour for more news.[17] Shafter doubted if he could hold his position at San Juan. He simply must hold it, they decided. They wired him so.

It was seven in the evening when the next news came in—terrifying news. Cervera's fleet, it said, had actually escaped from Santiago Harbor. Then, after a pause, came good news—the sinking of all but one of the enemy ships. But since it was not official the Presidential party remained at the White House in the hope of receiving official confirmation. They hovered over the wires all evening and into the night. At one o'clock in the morning of July 4 they received a dispatch from General Shafter reporting the actual destruction of Cervera's fleet. At two o'clock, when the Secretary of War left the White House, the newsboys were already out with the big story featured in the morning papers. In his pocket the Secretary carried some news that was not in the papers. It was another message from Shafter, brief but significant; it read: "I shall hold my present position." At noon on the nation's birthday Admiral Sampson's telegram was received: "The fleet under my command offers the nation, as a Fourth of July present, the whole of Cervera's fleet." [18]

The capture of Santiago was the next objective, but should it be by a direct assault or by siege? Shafter, because of the weakened condition of his army, did not favor either method. He proposed as the most effective means of taking Santiago that Sampson move his ships into Santiago Harbor and bombard it from the front while the army made a land attack. But the entrance to the harbor had been mined, and Sampson would not risk the

---

[17] Rhodes, p. 87.
[18] Millis, pp. 299–300, 314–15.

loss of his ships and his crews. The controversy arising between Sampson and Shafter resolved itself into a noisy battle of words between Secretary of War Alger and Secretary of the Navy Long at Washington. It proved to be a drawn-out Army-Navy battle which the President himself, when it was put up to him, could not settle.

Meanwhile Shafter engaged in a series of peace talks with the Spanish commander, General Toral. They were held midway between the opposing lines and beneath the sheltering branches of an enormous ciba tree, within sight of the American troops still occupying the trenches on San Juan Hill. With infinite patience the corpulent American general dickered with the procrastinating and at times exasperating Spaniard over the terms of surrender. Finally Toral offered to surrender Santiago on condition that his troops be allowed to march out of the city and take up their position at some other point. Shafter urged the President to accept the offer, but McKinley rejected Toral's terms and insisted upon an immediate and unconditional surrender. "What you went to Santiago for," the President declared in his reply to Shafter's message, "was the Spanish army. If you allow it to evacuate with its arms you must meet it somewhere else. This is not war. If the Spanish commander desires to leave the city and its people, let him surrender and we will then discuss the question as to what shall be done with them." [19] On July 17, two weeks after Cervera's defeat, articles of surrender on the basis of the President's terms were duly signed. On that day General Toral and his staff made a formal surrender of Santiago to Generals Shafter and Miles, accompanied by their military escorts.[20]

With the fall of Santiago hostilities in Cuba ceased. General Miles, who had a part in the negotiations leading to the surrender, was free to undertake the conquest of Porto Rico. He left Cuba soon after that historic event, taking with him over 3,400 men, mostly volunteers. Reinforcements during the campaign increased his army fivefold. With so large a force Miles

---

[19] Olcott, Vol. II, pp. 49–50.
[20] Millis, pp. 323–38.

and his staff were able to occupy much of Porto Rico before fighting was terminated by the armistice in August.[21]

On July 26 the American government received from the French ambassador in Washington a diplomatic note from Spain wishing to learn from the President on what terms peace could be had. To escape the hot weather of the capital the President and his Cabinet took a trip down the Potomac on board a lighthouse tender. They spent several days on board ship discussing Spain's note and drafting a reply. They were agreed as to most of the conditions that it should contain. The major difficulty was the Philippines.[22]

There the Filipino leader Aguinaldo, at the head of the native insurrectionists, had set up an independent Philippine Republic with himself as President. When the United States refused to recognize the new government and its head, Aguinaldo expressed great disappointment. On the eve of the capture of Manila by American troops the Filipino leader's attitude became so unfriendly that the United States was threatened with a probable insurrection by its former ally. Faced with such a prospect, some of McKinley's cabinet favored keeping all the Philippines rather than returning them to Spain. Some thought we should keep only a naval base. The President seemed undecided until a dispatch from Dewey informed him of Manila's impending surrender. Thereupon he decided to include as one of the terms in the peace protocol to Spain, "occupation by the United States of the city, bay and harbor of Manila pending the conclusion of a treaty of peace which shall determine the control, disposition and government of the Philippines." [23]

On July 30 the protocol in its final form was transmitted through the French ambassador to the Spanish government. On August 11 the American government was informed of Spain's acceptance, and on the next day, while the President stood looking on, the French ambassador and Secretary of State Day

---

[21] Latané, p. 58.

[22] Millis, p. 339.

[23] Latané, *America as a World Power*, p. 66 (all quotations by permission of Harper and Brothers).

signed the document that ended the war. Immediately after came
the President's proclamation terminating hostilities in every
theater of war.[24] Owing, however, to the absence of immediate
cable communication between Washington and the Philippines,
word of the armistice did not arrive until after the capture of
Manila and its surrender to the Americans.

The war lasted less than four months, but in that brief time
casualties from sickness and disease were heavy. By the end of
1898 nearly 3,500 had died of disease, as against fewer than 2,000
killed and wounded in action on all war fronts. The high death
toll from sickness became a leading topic of the sensational press.
Under flaming headlines the big dailies printed harrowing stories
about conditions in Cuba and the camps in the United States.
In high excitement over what they read in their papers the
American people vented their wrath on the War Department.
Secretary Alger was charged, often wrongly, with gross inefficiency and mismanagement.

In response to the hue and cry of the yellow press a camp for
convalescent soldiers was set up at Montauk Point on Long
Island. After urgent appeal by General Shafter most of the troops
in Cuba were ordered onto transports and taken to the new
camp. A stream of convalescent troops from other camps in the
country began flowing toward Montauk Point.[25]

Before preparations for removing the army from Cuba were
completed, however, the newspapers came out with another sen-
sation, a real scoop by the Associated Press. A document known
as the Round Robin had been drafted and signed by members
of General Shafter's staff. Although it was addressed to Shafter,
it was turned over to the Associated Press for publication without his knowledge or authorization. It contained a shocking
revelation of the condition of the army in Cuba and insisted
upon its immediate removal to the United States. Unless this
were done, the army would perish.[26]

To the President, who knew nothing at all of its existence,

---

[24] Oberholtzer, Vol. V, p. 549.
[25] Oberholtzer, Vol. V, pp. 554–57.
[26] Oberholtzer, Vol. V, pp. 553–55.

the document when published in the Washington papers was a
bolt from the blue. It was a clear case of military insubordina-
tion, and since it came while our government was awaiting
Spain's compliance with the terms of the peace protocol it
proved to be extremely embarrassing. Neither did it serve any
good purpose. Authorities at Washington were well aware from
Shafter's reports of the serious situation in Cuba and had already
taken steps to remedy it.

The Round Robin affair only intensified the criticism of Secretary Alger, and the public clamor for his removal became deaf-
ening. The term "Algerism" was coined and circulated over the
country in token of the dislike felt for the unfortunate War Department head. The President, also, was placed in a painful
position. Although Alger had become a political liability to the
administration, McKinley was reluctant, for reasons of loyalty
and friendship, to oust him from the Cabinet. Fearing the effect
that "Algerism" might have on the midterm elections in the fall,
McKinley appointed a nine-man commission to conduct an investigation of the War Department.[27] The commission traveled
about in search of evidence, examined many witnesses, and collected volumes of testimony. Among the many matters looked
into were charges made by Major-General Miles that much of
the canned beef sold the War Department by the meat-packers
was impure and had been chemically treated. This, Miles
charged, was largely responsible for sickness among soldiers in
the camps and Cuba. In the judgment of the commission, after
it had completed its hearings on the Miles case, the general had
failed to substantiate his charges. In other particulars, too, the
report was generally favorable. Since this was apparently not
what the public expected and wanted to hear, the report was
condemned as "whitewash." The investigation did nothing to
silence public criticism. The people, egged on by the sensational
press, continued to cry out for Alger's dismissal.[28]

One fact had to be faced. The war and its problems had
demonstrated beyond any doubt that the War Department was

---

[27] Oberholtzer, Vol. V, p. 559.
[28] Olcott, Vol. II, p. 83.

in need of reorganization, and this perception made a change of administration inevitable. Eventually Alger would have to go. But he did not offer to retire, and the President, in spite of all the public outcry, did not ask for his resignation. The sentiment of the press by that time was almost universal in demanding a change.

At length, in the spring of 1899, an opportunity to make a change presented itself. Alger's continuance in the McKinley Cabinet was made impossible when he became a candidate for United States Senator from Michigan, actively supported by the governor of that state, who was openly opposed to the McKinley administration. His resignation was requested by Vice-President Hobart, to whom that unpleasant task was assigned.[29]

For his successor the President turned to an Easterner, Elihu Root of New York. But before asking Root to take the War portfolio, he made sure that his appointment had the approval of the powerful Republican boss of New York, Senator Platt. Platt's position in the Senate was such that he could block Root's appointment if he chose. Moreover, some appeasement of him was necessary, for by retiring Alger, who happened to be Platt's intimate friend, the President had ruffled the temper of the New York Senator.[30]

When asked to take the War secretaryship Root at first declined with the plea that he knew nothing about war or the Army. But that, he was told, was immaterial. The President wanted him because he needed a lawyer like Root to advise him about the new colonial possessions. Thereupon the New York lawyer agreed to accept the United States as his client.[31]

Root proved to be a valuable accession to the McKinley Cabinet. He had already won a national reputation as a lawyer as a result of a long and varied legal practice in his native state.

---

[29] Olcott, Vol. II, p. 89.

[30] P. C. Jessup, *Elihu Root*, Vol. I, pp. 215–16.

[31] Two years before, McKinley had wanted to appoint Root United States minister to Spain during the diplomatic crisis over Cuba. As an inducement the President offered him an ambassadorship, but Root refused the offer because he feared that he could not serve acceptably (Jessup, Vol. I, p. 196).

He had never shown much interest in politics, and only once had he been a candidate for elective office: he had run for judge of the Court of Common Pleas in New York in 1878 and been defeated.[32] The only public office Root had held before becoming Secretary of War under McKinley was that of United States Attorney for the Southern District of New York, to which he was appointed by his intimate friend President Arthur.[33]

---

[32] Jessup, Vol. I, pp. 117–18.
[33] Jessup, Vol. I, pp. 136–37.

CHAPTER XVI

Republican Peace and Imperialism

In accordance with the peace protocol President McKinley on August 26 named five men to a commission to negotiate a treaty of peace with a like number of commissioners from Spain. At the head of the commission he placed Secretary of State Day. Three of the commissioners were Senators and members of the Senate Foreign Relations Committee: Kushman Davis, Chairman, W. P. Frye, ranking Republican member, and George Gray, leading Democratic member. The fifth man was Whitelaw Reid, editor of the New York *Tribune*, which had turned expansionist in tone. Reid's expansionism was shown in a recent article of his advocating that all the Philippines be retained. Davis and Frye were known to be strongly for expansion; Gray held contrary views. As for Day, his reluctance to annex the Philippines as a whole seemed to place him about midway between the other commissioners. The commission was to be in Paris on October 1.[1]

Before setting forth, the commissioners met with the President and his Cabinet in several conferences to consider the delicate subject of the Philippines. The political aspects of the problem were rendered difficult by the divided state of public

---

[1] Millis, p. 372; Latané, p. 68.

opinion in the United States. In the official instructions to the commissioners the abandonment of Spain's possessions in the Western Hemisphere was insisted upon in the interest of permanent peace. No other course was therefore open than to demand the cession of Cuba, Porto Rico, and other islands held by Spain in that hemisphere. The Philippines were in a different category. But the conquest and occupation of Manila by American arms, it was felt, had brought inevasible duties and responsibilities to the United States. Therefore, the President concluded, the commission should insist as a minimum demand upon the full cession of the island of Luzon.[2]

The peace commission arrived in Paris on September 26 and was received by French Foreign Minister Delcasse. At a luncheon on the next day the American commission met the members of the Spanish commission. On October 1 negotiations were opened at the Quai d'Orsay. Three days later General Merrit, direct from the Philippines, appeared at the conference. As one who had been actively engaged at Manila in events leading to its surrender, he gave the commissioners the benefit of his views. They also heard from other Army and Navy officers and from writers and travelers who had information on the Islands.

It was not, however, over the Philippines that the negotiations began. For the first two weeks the conference was in an impasse as a result of Spain's demand that the United States, in accepting sovereignty, should also take over with it the debt incurred by Spain during the Cuban Wars, the same to be assumed either by the United States or Cuba. Day's opinion as expressed in a letter to the President was that the debt represented the investment of many Spanish landholders who hoped in this way to recover some of their losses.[3] The American commission reluctantly denied the basis of Spain's contention. They took the position that the debts she wished to unload on the United States were obligations not owed by Cuba, but rather incurred by Spain while endeavoring to crush the Cuban struggle for more self-government and eventual independence—the struggle that had led to

---

[2] Olcott, Vol. II, pp. 95–96.
[3] Olcott, Vol. II, p. 99.

American intervention and to war.[4] In reply the Spaniards proposed that the Cuban debt be settled by arbitration, and when this was rejected they threatened to break off negotiations. Whitelaw Reid, writing to the President, was inclined to think that Spain's commission was in danger of being ordered home because of a cabinet crisis at Madrid. Probably because of the timely intervention of Castillo, the Spanish ambassador at Paris, through an interview with Reid, a complete breakdown of negotiations was averted.[5] In any event, on the next day the Spanish commission agreed to give in to the American demand, seemingly in the vain hope, held before them by the Spanish ambassador, of gaining some substantial advantage in negotiating over the Philippines.

Firmly united as they were on the Cuban debt, the American commissioners were seriously divided for a time on the Philippine problem. On October 25 they cabled their views to the President, who had just returned from his western trip. Davis, Frye, and Reid were convinced the entire archipelago should be taken over; Day was for taking only Luzon and a handful of strategic islands. Senator Gray stood out against his colleagues by rejecting entirely the idea of annexing the Philippines as a whole or in part.[6] In answer to their request for explicit instructions the President directed Secretary of State Hay (who had now succeeded Day) to cable a dispatch plainly conveying a change in point of view on his part. The President, it was stated, on the basis of information received since their departure for Paris was convinced that the acceptance of "the cession of Luzon alone

---

[4] Millis questions the ethical soundness of the American position. "For thirty years," as he puts the case, "we had been officially urging the Spanish Government to bend its every effort toward the suppression of these outbreaks; while at the same time, it was by no means certain that we ourselves were prepared to admit that the insurgent patriots represented the hopes and aspirations of the body of the Cuban people" (p. 378).

[5] Olcott, Vol. II, pp. 104–5.

[6] Gray held that to annex the Philippines would be contrary to American continental policy and would involve the United States in Europe's entangling alliances and politics, against which Washington had cautioned. Moreover, in demanding the Philippines the United States was slipping down from the high and noble plane assumed when the war began.

. . . cannot be justified on political, commercial, or humanitarian grounds. The cession must be the whole archipelago or none. The latter is wholly inadmissible and the former must therefore be required." [7] The President's stand as indicated by Secretary Hay's supplementary instructions was that while, as victors, we should hold only to motives that would exalt us as a nation, territorial acquisition being our lesser concern, we must not shrink from our moral obligations as victors. The Philippines could be claimed on the basis of conquest, but the President preferred that their cession by Spain should follow as a result of negotiations according to the protocol. [8]

The task of reconciling such apparently contradictory ideas to the satisfaction of the Spanish peacemakers proved most difficult. In pressing for the surrender of the Philippines on the basis of conquest our commissioners felt that they were on dubious ground. There was truth in Spain's contention that, since Manila had fallen after August 12, the date of the protocol, the Americans did not hold any part of the islands by conquest. Day, in a letter to the President, stated that in his judgment the Americans had under international law no right to possession by conquest. If, then, such a claim was untenable, by what legal process could the cession of the Philippines be required? [9] These views as set forth in Day's letter were also shared by his colleagues. They were clearly convinced that they had no real basis for demanding the islands, and one of them, Senator Frye, feared that if such a demand were pressed the negotiations might break down without securing a treaty. But the President remained unmoved. The conquest of Manila, he insisted, occurred with the destruction of the Spanish fleet in Manila Bay. [10]

When, as might have been foreseen, the Spaniards flatly turned down the demand for the Philippines, another serious deadlock followed. But out of it emerged an idea that, strangely enough, found its way into the final draft of the treaty. Why not,

---

[7] Latané, pp. 71–72.
[8] Millis, p. 385.
[9] Olcott, Vol. II, pp. 114 ff.
[10] Latané, p. 73.

in order to secure a treaty, propose taking the Philippines as indemnity, but pay Spain a few millions to reimburse her for her expenditures in the islands? Agreed as to the necessity of such a proposal, the commission cabled the President and urged its acceptance. On November 13 came instructions from Secretary Hay authorizing the cession of the Philippines and the payment of ten to twenty millions to Spain, the cession to include a naval station in the Carolines.[11] The President's concern, the commissioners were informed by the Secretary, was that the treaty should be one "which would not only satisfy the present generation but, what is more important, be justified in the judgment of posterity."[12] Meanwhile, in Paris, Commissioner Reid and his colleagues anxiously waited for word from Washington. The Paris newspapers, Reid informed the President in his letter of November 15, were predicting that peace negotiations would fail. There was much talk circulating to the effect that there would be no treaty. The Spanish commission gave that as their opinion, and the Americans were being influenced by such stories. "About one day in three," Reid wrote, "I find myself accepting these stories. On the other two, I still hope for a treaty." On the basis of inside news from Madrid Reid felt sure that the Spanish Queen Regent, realizing that nothing more could be gained for her once proud empire, would be ready to face the inevitable. Prime Minister Sagasta shrank from making a decision that would banish him from power for good.[13]

Hay's instructions were at once transmitted to the Spaniards, who were given two days to reply. But still they yearned to put off the evil day, and they stalled for time in the desperate hope of raising the sum to be paid or perhaps gaining one or two more concessions. Several days passed before word authorizing acceptance of the terms came; and it was not until November 30 that the final draft of the treaty was begun. But when Congress convened in Washington five days later, the Spanish commission still lingered over details of the draft, while the Americans, fear-

---

[11] Olcott, Vol. II, p. 119.
[12] Oberholtzer, Vol. V, p. 576.
[13] Olcott, Vol. II, pp. 125–26.

ful for the treaty, stood impatiently looking on.[14] Finally, on December 10, the formal signing of the document took place. The articles stipulated for the cession to the United States of Cuba, Porto Rico, and all other remaining islands in the West Indies, Guam of the Ladrones, and the Philippines, for which $20,000,000 was to be paid within three months after exchange of treaty ratifications.

The ratification of the treaty, as was generally foreseen, involved a turning point in the nation's career, a break with traditions long accepted and honored as truly American. Such hesitations were bound to be asserted when the din and tumult of battle were over and the moment came for the nation to study seriously and calmly the prospect that lay ahead. The conclusion of the treaty was followed by a lively discussion by the press of the imperialistic course which the new school of political thinkers was advocating for America. In the Senate discussion erupted almost immediately after Congress met in December, and it continued into the new year for a month after the treaty had been submitted by the President to be ratified.

Senate debate was started by a resolution introduced by Senator Vest of Missouri on December 6, to the effect that the Federal government did not have constitutional authority to acquire territory to be held or governed as permanent colonies. Under the Constitution, the Senator argued, we are restricted to acquiring territory that could be organized into states.[15] While Senator Platt of Connecticut spoke strongly against the Vest resolution, Senator Hoar of Massachusetts presented a powerful argument in its favor. Platt, in favoring ratification of the treaty, held that the United States as a nation had inherent sovereign power both to acquire and to govern territory. Such a contention, however, was hard to reconcile with the principle clearly set forth in the Constitution that the Federal government is a government of delegated and not inherent powers.[16] Speaking in opposition to

---

[14] Millis, pp. 388–89. Since the treaty had not been concluded when the President's message was sent to Congress, it made no reference to the islands to be acquired from Spain, with the exception of Cuba.

[15] Millis, p. 394.

[16] Latané, p. 75.

For the next two years systematic efforts to repair the wreckage and devastation in the war-torn island were made. In his report on Cuba General Fitzhugh Lee drew a graphic picture of conditions. Business and agriculture were paralyzed; property everywhere was in ruins; miles of open country had been abandoned by man and beast, and in the cities the sick, the famished, and the destitute survived in desperation. Free though they were of Spain's inhuman rule, the people were filled with apprehension.

During 1899 shiploads of food from the United States were landed and distributed to Cubans facing starvation. Those able to work were given employment. Cuban troops numbering nearly 50,000 were disbanded and paid cash bounties. A determined, efficient fight against sickness and disease was waged. The first steps to eradicate the dreaded yellow fever were taken. By means of sanitation Cuba was made safe for human occupancy. Hospitals and medical care were provided. New road construction and repair of old roads made communication and travel once more possible, meanwhile giving work to thousands of Cubans in need of means of support.

A vigorous assault was also waged against ignorance and illiteracy, the wide prevalence of which was revealed by a census taken in 1900. Millions of American dollars went into new schools, schoolbooks, and supplies. Cubans were encouraged to come to the United States to enroll as students in courses for training teachers.[2] Such were some of the measures for cutting down the two-thirds illiteracy of the Cuban population.

The progress thus made took place under two military governors, Major-General Brooke and his successor, General Leonard Wood. In September, 1900, delegates to a constitutional convention were elected, the ballot being restricted to Cubans and Spaniards pledged to become Cuban citizens and able to meet certain literacy and property tests. The convention met in Havana in November, General Wood acting as presiding officer. It drafted a constitution for a republican form of government similar to that of the United States. But the delegates were jeal-

---

[2] Olcott, Vol. II, pp. 202–6.

ous of Cuba's sovereignty and showed themselves unfriendly to proposals to limit Cuban independence. Before completing its work on the constitution the convention was obliged to include a provision known as the Platt Amendment. This measure, designed to safeguard Cuban independence, placed certain limitations on the young republic's foreign relations. When adopted in June, 1901, the Platt Amendment virtually made Cuba a protectorate of its powerful neighbor to the north.[3] President McKinley did not live to see the consummation of his plans for Cuba's reconstruction; the election of its first President and Vice-President and the transfer of governing authority into their hands did not take place until 1902.

In one important respect, however, Cuban rehabilitation fell short of expectations. Scandalous mismanagement of the Cuban postal department by dishonest American officials reflected badly on the integrity of the administration. Attention was first called to the malfeasance of these officials by their extravagant style of living while residing in Havana. Suspicion that they were doubtless living beyond their means led to an investigation of the Cuban postal system. Inspectors sent to Cuba to make a probe soon returned with startling reports of inefficiency and graft. The guilty parties, it was disclosed, had defrauded the Cubans of about $130,000, or more than a third of the gross postal revenue.[4]

It was just another sordid tale of official misconduct growing out of the war with Spain. But the serious nature of the incident in the eyes of the President was the betrayal of Cuba's trust in the honesty of those appointed to act for this country as Cuba's protector.[5]

The situation in Porto Rico was such that in the judgment of McKinley and his advisers it called for special consideration.

---

[3] Under the terms of the Platt Amendment to the Army Appropriations Act of 1901, Cuba must not permit foreign powers to impair her sovereign independence, must not incur debt in excess of her financial resources, must grant the express right of the United States to intervene to protect Cuban independence, and must allow the United States to hold naval bases on the island (Latané, pp. 176–81).

[4] Bristow, pp. 102 ff.

[5] Bristow, p. 100.

Economically, Porto Rico depended almost entirely on foreign markets. The recent war had entirely cut off its trade with Spain and other Spanish possessions. To make matters worse, the high Dingley tariff duties on sugar and tobacco had practically closed American markets to these products of Porto Rico. As President McKinley made clear in his message to Congress in December, 1899, Porto Rico had lost the Spanish and Cuban outlets on which it had been dependent, while getting no concessions in American markets to compensate. "The markets of the United States, therefore," the President urged, "should be opened up to her products. Our plain duty is to abolish all custom tariffs between the United States and Porto Rico and give her products free access to our markets." [6]

The President's recommendation that Porto Rico be included within the tariff lines of the United States was accepted by Congress and made part of the Porto Rican revenue bill. Very soon stiff resistance was made by American cane sugar, beet sugar, and tobacco growers, who feared a deluge of Porto Rican sugar and tobacco if they were admitted free of duty. They demanded that a protective tariff be placed on these products, and with such insistence that the President saw fit to reverse himself. He now perceived that American interests must not be jeopardized for the sake of Porto Rico. It would not do to run counter to Republican protectionist desires and thereby cause a split in the party. "We need party harmony on the greater and more important question of the Philippines," he said to a close friend. "I know I shall be charged with weakness, but I prefer to endure any such charges rather than face the future with a disunited party." [7]

Accordingly, members of the House were personally urged by the President to vote for a duty on Porto Rican products equal to 25 per cent of the Dingley rates. As a result of much criticism, however, the duty was cut to 15 per cent when, in February, 1900, the bill was passed.

---

[6] J. D. Richardson, *Messages and Papers of the Presidents*, Vol. XIII, p. 6403.

[7] Olcott, Vol. II, p. 218.

The Foraker Bill, providing for civil government in Porto Rico, was tied to the House Tariff Bill as an amendment and made law. As such, it stipulated that the 15-per-cent duty on Porto Rican products would be effective only until March 1, 1902, and that all revenue collected under it until that date would be paid over to Porto Rico.[8]

The constitution embodied in the Foraker Act differed essentially from every previous form of territorial government established by Congress. A governor and an executive council of eleven members were made appointive by the President and Senate. The council was made the upper branch of the legislature, six of its members to be Americans, each of whom was to be the head of an administrative department. Five of the council were to be native Porto Ricans. The lower lawmaking branch consisted of thirty-five delegates elected biennially by qualified voters. To Congress was given the power to amend or annul legislation passed by the council and governor that lacked its approval. Franchises granted by the executive council and governor must be approved by Congress. The Porto Ricans, since they lacked powers of self-government and their island had no legal status as either a territory or a state, looked upon themselves as inhabitants without a country. Under the Foraker Act they were made citizens of Porto Rico.[9]

In the Philippines much had to be done to bring the islands up to the standards set for them. Through the reports of a commission headed by President J. G. Schurman of Cornell University, which had visited the islands and compiled a useful survey of conditions there, much of the appalling ignorance in America concerning them was being dispelled. The chief difficulty was the full-scale insurrection under Aguinaldo, centering mainly in southern Luzon, largest of the group. The American

---

[8] When Senator Hanna was asked why he voted for the Foraker Bill with the 15-per-cent duty, his reply as reported was: "I'll tell you exactly. We received notice from 250,000 Union cigar rollers that if we admitted Porto Rican cigars free of duty, each of the 250,000 would get three other union men to vote against the Republican party in November, 1900, making 1,000,000 votes against McKinley" (Kohlsaat, p. 71).

[9] Walters, p. 170; Latané, p. 141.

commanders MacArthur, Otis, and Lawton, with about 50,000 troops, were capturing positions held by insurrectionists, forcing them northward, and putting their leaders to flight. In December, 1899, convinced that future organized resistance was useless, Aguinaldo disbanded his army and prepared to undertake a campaign of guerrilla warfare. For two long years the Filipino guerrillas fought the Americans, employing tactics of extreme ferocity and cruelty, which the American troops often imitated in reprisal. But in spite of guerrilla atrocities, American casualties from May, 1900, to July, 1901, were slight compared with those of the enemy.[10]

Meantime Aguinaldo was captured by means of a clever ruse. His capture did not, as was hoped, slow down the insurrection, especially outside of Luzon. In the islands of Mindoro, Samar, Cebu, and Bohol, American troops met with open resistance. But the back of the insurrection was broken by 1902 with the firm occupation of the islands and their surrender to the occupying armies.[11] In the United States much criticism was stirred up by newspapers that played up the Philippine struggle as a savage and ruthless war to subjugate a weaker people. The insurgents had many American sympathizers, but American sentiment in general rallied behind the administration.[12]

Before the insurrection had run its course President McKinley picked another five-man commission with William H. Taft at its head. Its assignment was to go to the Philippines and, on the basis of existing local conditions, establish civil government, first in the local communities and then on a large scale in the provinces. A central civil government over the Philippines was to be imposed at such time as the commission thought proper. It had legislative power; executive authority was vested in General MacArthur, the military governor. The resultant system was a government partly civil, partly military, and subject to the President as commander-in-chief. Under what was known as the Spooner Amendment, of March, 1901, the President was given

---

[10] Latané, pp. 96–97.
[11] Latané, pp. 97–98.
[12] Oberholtzer, pp. 596–97.

a broad scope of power over the newly established organization, by means of which he was able to complete the separation of the civil from the military functions—a separation already begun by the Taft Commission. As a consequence, by July 4, 1901, in accordance with a Presidential proclamation, Taft as civil governor assumed the executive power formerly held by the military governor. His authority included appointment of civil officeholders with the commission's consent. Shortly before McKinley's death in September the Philippine Commission was enlarged by the addition of three Filipino members. Four executive departments were created and members of the commission placed over them.[13]

In a general way Cuba and the Philippines presented somewhat parallel situations. American troops were sent to the Philippines, as to Cuba, to liberate them from Spain's oppressive rule and to occupy the islands after conquering them. The Filipinos, like the Cubans, aspired to be an independent nation. Aided by the United States, they hoped to win their independence and govern themselves under a republic of which Aguinaldo declared himself the head. When the United States refused to recognize the republic or Aguinaldo, the effect was to make his followers insurrectionists against the United States, and the war to liberate the Filipinos became a war to crush the insurrectionists.

Long before this stage any analogy between Cuba and the Philippines, so far as the United States was concerned, had ceased. The President's critics, however, persisted in asking why, instead of keeping the Filipinos under American control without their consent, the islands were not returned to them to be governed by them under their own system as an independent nation. As a necessary precaution to safeguard their independence, a protectorate could be set over them as had been done in Cuba. Against such proposals the President spoke with convincing force. He maintained that the establishment of stable government in the Philippines meant that they must be under the sovereign authority and flag of the United States. "As the

---

[13] Latané, pp. 157–60.

sovereign power," he declared, "we can initiate action and shape means to ends, and guide the Filipinos to self-development and self-government. As a protectorate power we could not initiate action but would be compelled to follow and uphold a people with no capacity to go alone. In the one case we can protect both ourselves and the Filipinos from being involved in dangerous complications; in the other we could not protect even the Filipinos until after their trouble had come. Besides, if we cannot establish any government of our own without the consent of the governed, as our opponents contend, then we could not establish a stable government for them or make ours a protectorate without the like consent, and neither the majority of the people nor a minority of the people have invited us to assume it. We could not maintain a protectorate even with the consent of the governed without giving provocation for conflicts and possible wars." [14]

The Hawaiian Islands were annexed by joint resolution of Congress in July, 1898, after a treaty providing for their annexation had been rejected by the Senate. American interest in Hawaii extended back to the time when Pearl Harbor, near Honolulu, was secured as a naval station under a lease from the Hawaiian government. Meanwhile many Americans, attracted by the delightful climate and other advantages of the islands, had become residents. By 1890 American capital invested in Hawaiian sugar plantations amounted to $25,000,000. The importance of the Hawaiian Islands to the United States for naval purposes was heightened after the outbreak of the war with Spain, especially after the battle of Manila and subsequent military operations in the Philippines.

Hawaii, in marked contrast to the islands acquired from Spain, presented no complications. The inhabitants had clearly demonstrated their ability to govern themselves. They had set up a republic of their own, capable of maintaining law and order at home and winning the respect of other nations. For the President their long-deferred annexation meant no change in our

---

[14] Letter of acceptance of nomination as Republican candidate for President, September 8, 1900.

system. It was merely a consummation. Unlike Porto Rico and the Philippines, which according to the courts were not territories but dependencies of the United States, this mid-Pacific archipelago was given territorial status by Congress. Under a law enacted in April, 1900, Congress expressly extended to them the Constitution of the United States, and all persons who were citizens of Hawaii, when transferred to the United States, were to become citizens of the United States. Under the same act the Hawaiians were organized as a territory.[15]

When McKinley in his message of December, 1899, urged that Porto Rico be included in the tariff laws of the United States, he did so on the theory that the Constitution and laws of the United States extended automatically over the island as a territory. By authority of the constitutional clause requiring that all duties, imposts, and excises be uniform throughout the United States, the President had asked that tariffs between that country and Porto Rico be abolished and its products admitted free of duty. But, yielding to the pressure of powerful political interests demanding protection against Porto Rican sugar and tobacco, he aligned himself with them and came out strongly for a duty. Constitutionally this placed him on different ground. For, if Porto Rico were only a dependency and not a territory of the United States, then it could not be included under the constitutional provision as to uniformity of duties and imposts unless Congress by law specifically so declared, and until that time its trade with the United States would be subject to the collection of duties.

The Foraker and the Porto Rican tariff acts raised a tempest of controversy in the nation concerning the constitutional position of Porto Rico in relation to the United States. In the popular language of that day, does the Constitution follow the flag? Congress and the President answered in the affirmative. It rested with the judiciary to express an opinion. In the fall of 1900 a series of suits, the insular cases, were carried to the Supreme Court on appeal. They involved the legal right to collect duties

---

[15] Walters, p. 170; Latané, pp. 141–43.

on imports of goods from the newly acquired possessions. In several instances, the appellants brought suit to recover duties paid under protest on imports from Porto Rico. In one case, De Lima *vs.* Bidwell, a majority of the justices ruled that, since Porto Rico after its cession to the United States was not a foreign country, its trade was not subject to the Dingley tariff. Therefore duties paid on sugar imported from Porto Rico were illegally imposed and collected and must be returned to the importers. In a dissenting opinion a minority of the court held that, since Porto Rico's position with reference to the United States was neither that of a foreign country nor that of a domestic territory over which the Dingley tariff extended, Porto Rican products were subject to that law and the duties were legally collectible.[16]

According to an opinion by a majority of the judges in the case of Downs *vs.* Bidwell, Porto Rico when ceded became a territory belonging to the United States, but not a part thereof to which the revenue clauses of the Constitution were applicable. The collection of duties on imports from that island under the Foraker Act was therefore declared to be within the constitutional power of Congress. Four of the nine judges joined in a dissenting opinion. The majority opinion was made possible only by the fact that the judge who read the majority opinion of the court in the first case had changed his position in the second case, though his decision was reached by a process of reasoning that none of his colleagues accepted.[17]

On the constitutional position of the insular possessions in relation to the United States the Supreme Court's opinion no doubt contained much that to the public was confusing and contradictory. Yet, however hazy and vague the popular impression, a few facts seemed to stand forth clearly enough. Porto Rico and

---

[16] Latané, pp. 144–45.

[17] For the arguments of the judges, see Latané, pp. 146–50. In the Fourteen Diamond Rings Case of December, 1901, in which the same issue as that raised in the De Lima–Bidwell Case was involved, the court concluded that the Philippine Islands when transferred to the United States ceased to be foreign territory and that goods brought from them to the United States were not subject to a tariff.

the Philippines were not territories but dependencies over which the provisions of the Constitution and laws of the United States did not extend until Congress by special legislation saw fit to make those dependencies subject to them—power that Congress had and could exercise. The Porto Ricans and the Filipinos were not citizens of the United States and did not possess the rights and privileges of citizenship. Though hesitatingly, the Court had decided in favor of the imperialistic course pursued by the McKinley administration. It gave its approval to the measures taken by that administration in order to set the nation's feet firmly on the path to empire. In a time when the government was undergoing great and fundamental change the Court yielded to change as an accomplished fact. To have done otherwise, especially after the nation itself had given at the polls its unmistakable approval of the march of events since 1898, would have caused grave confusion and uncertainty. In the words of a famous humorist of the time, writing as Mr. Dooley: "No matter whether the Constitution follows the flag or not, the Supreme Court follows the illiction returns." [18]

---

[18] Oberholtzer, p. 672*n*.

CHAPTER XVIII

Postwar Diplomacy

The American State Department in its diplomatic relations with other governments generally had President McKinley's firm support. This was plainly manifested in connection with two major subjects of diplomacy that claimed the department's attention following the Spanish War: the construction of a canal through Central America and some developments in China.

American interest in an artificial waterway somewhere through Central America, and particularly one that would be exclusively an American waterway, was running high near the turn of the century. In response to it the United States Senate had passed a bill early in 1899 authorizing the construction of an American-owned canal through the isthmus of Nicaragua. In the meantime the Panama Canal Company had sent a lobby to Washington to stir up interest in Congress in the isthmus of Panama as a desirable site for such a project. The President, authorized by Congress, appointed a commission headed by Admiral J. G. Walker to investigate all possible routes through Central America and to report its findings to Congress.[1]

The Walker Commission in its report to Congress on Novem-

---

[1] Tyler Dennett, *John Hay*, pp. 226–27.

ber 30, 1900, declared its preference for the Nicaragua route. Securing the necessary rights, privileges, and franchises covering that route, the Commission reported, would be less difficult than in Panama. Moreover, the cost of constructing a canal by way of Panama would be greater because of the price the Panama Company would demand for the sale of its property.[2]

Meantime Secretary of State Hay, taking advantage of the cordial friendship between his government and the British, set about negotiating a treaty that should supersede the outdated Clayton-Bulwer Convention of 1850. The new agreement, known as the first Hay-Pauncefote Treaty, granted the United States sole right to build and operate a canal through Central America, but did not in so many words stipulate repeal of the Clayton-Bulwer Treaty. By reason of this deficiency the document encountered stiff opposition when sent to the Senate to be ratified. To Hay's dismay, several amendments were added, including one that provided for the express abrogation of the unpopular Convention of fifty years before. Bitterly disappointed, aware that the amended treaty would not be acceptable to the British, and fearing that his own usefulness as Secretary was at an end, Hay tendered his resignation to the President. In a letter to Hay assuring him of his staunch support, McKinley declared: "Your administration of the State Department has had my warm approval. As in all matters you have taken my counsel, I will cheerfully bear whatever criticism or condemnation may come. Your record constitutes one of the most important and interesting pages of our diplomatic history." [3]

Heartened by the assured backing of his chief, Hay again took up negotiations with Lord Pauncefote. Another treaty was drafted and signed by November 18, 1901. One month later it was ratified by the Senate. Although it definitely provided for the abrogation of the Clay-Bulwer Treaty, it was accepted by the British government. Its silence as to the right of the United

---

[2] Olcott, Vol. I, pp. 371–72.

[3] W. R. Thayer, *Life and Letters of John Hay,* Vol. II, p. 226 (quoted by permission of the Houghton Mifflin Company).

States to fortify the proposed canal seemed to imply that the British had also withdrawn their objection to such a provision of the first Hay-Pauncefote Treaty.[4] The ratification of the second treaty consummated another significant move in the McKinley program for American control of the Caribbean from Key West to Central America. Two previous major moves to that end had been the annexation of Porto Rico and the Platt Amendment giving the United States a protectorate over Cuba, thereby enabling it to demand the naval bases and coaling stations needed to safeguard the approaches to the projected waterway, over which the United States would have exclusive control.

The timely possession of the Philippines enabled the United States also to play a decisive role in the developments occurring at a startling pace in eastern Asia. China's defeat by Japan laid bare her appalling weakness to the world and soon brought the Powers to the scene like greedy vultures about a carcass. Each Power staked off a Chinese coastal area as its "sphere of influence" or seized outright certain portions of the Chinese littoral to be exploited for its own special benefit. For the United States to have engaged in this game of grab would have been utterly at variance with our traditions. Nevertheless our nearness to China and the possible ruin of American trade by these developments made it imperative to establish some constructive policy suited to a situation that, if continued, might result in China's complete dismemberment.

The initial impulse that made the American government act apparently came from Great Britain. In March, 1898, while the President was being pressured by Congress to intervene in Cuba, he received from the British ambassador a memorandum requesting to know if the United States would go along with his government in a joint declaration opposing the European Powers in China and urging the continuance of equal world trade with that nation. The President's reply, made through the State Department, was not encouraging. He apparently saw nothing in the situation that might endanger American interests, or at any rate

---

[4] Rhodes, pp. 262–63.

nothing that should cause the United States to depart from its traditional stand against foreign alliances. In answer to a letter from Hay, then ambassador in London, suggesting that the British proposal be considered, the President again replied through the State Department in effect that he regarded the suggestion as inopportune.[5]

But the British, and apparently many Americans as well, did not look at the matter in that light. From Lord Beresford, a representative of the associated Chambers of Commerce who had toured in the Orient, Hay learned that Americans in that part of the globe were "most sympathetic" to the idea of a commercial alliance with England based on the integrity of China and the open door for all nations' trade. Since American trade in northern China was very lucrative, Beresford expressed confidence that such an alliance would materialize.[6]

Early in 1899 the British attempted once more to reopen the subject of an Anglo-American alliance based, in the words of Lord Pauncefote, on the "special community of interests" of both countries in China. However much the proposal may have appealed to the American Secretary of State, he withheld assent, declaring such an alliance to be "positively forbidden to us by both the Senate and public opinion." [7]

No definite stand was taken by the United States with respect to China until the late summer of 1899, when Hay formulated his celebrated notes on the Open Door, the underlying principles of which were apparently of British derivation. According to one writer much of their substance was suggested to Hay by an English customs inspector in China, A. E. Hippisley, with whom the Secretary and his chief adviser, W. W. Rockhill, were in consultation.[8] Another authority has stated that the ideas on the Open Door were suggested to Hay by Lord Beresford while on a trip through the United States and incorporated in a mem-

[5] Dennett, pp. 285–86.

[6] Dennett, p. 286.

[7] Dennett, p. 288 (all quotations by permission of Dodd, Mead and Company).

[8] Dennett, pp. 290–91.

orandum drafted by Rockhill at Hay's request.[9] In any event, American policy guaranteeing the territorial integrity of China and the Open Door was thus made effective, not by joint action or by alliances or formal treaties, which the President did not favor, but by simple, informal understandings with each of the several Powers concerned. In this form, Hay's position received the President's unqualified support.

The Boxer uprising of 1900 opened the way for enlarging the new China policy. Led by a group of fanatics, the people of North China rose in protest against the presence of foreigners in an anti-foreign demonstration meant to rid China of the "foreign devils." By June the Boxers, with the secret support of the Empress Dowager, took Peking and besieged the British legation there, to which most of the foreigners had fled for refuge. During a siege that lasted until August 14, when a joint military expedition came to the relief of the beleaguered city, all contact was cut off and it was generally assumed that all of those inside the city had been murdered.[10]

That a situation so intensely critical came to a happy ending was largely due to Hay's skillful diplomacy. He had undertaken the twofold task of rescuing the besieged in Peking and keeping the Powers from seizing the opportunity to wrest more concessions from China. Since it was an important election year, political considerations narrowly hampered his efforts. In order to prevent the relief expeditionary force from turning into a large-scale military enterprise against China, Hay induced the Powers to join his government in localizing the insurrection. In a diplomatic circular issued on July 3, 1900, he announced that it was the sincere desire of the United States "to remain at peace and friendship with the people of China." Our policy was "to seek a solution which may bring about permanent safety and peace in China, preserve China's territorial and administrative entity, protect all rights guaranteed to friendly Powers by treaty and international law and safeguard for the world, the principle of equal

---

[9] Allan Nevins, *Henry White: Thirty Years of American Diplomacy*, p. 166.

[10] Latané, p. 105.

and impartial trade with all parts of the Chinese Empire." [11]

President McKinley, concerned for the safety of the legations in Peking, agreed to send American troops to China on a rescue mission in co-operation with the other Powers. His decision, made in Canton, Ohio, was reached after a telephone conversation with Secretary of War Root in Washington. On the Secretary's advice it was decided to organize an American army made up of several regiments previously withdrawn from Cuba, Porto Rico, and the Philippines. [12] By early August the allied army, composed of Japanese, Russian, British, French, and American soldiers, set out on the first expedition of the kind in which Americans had participated. It marched from Tientsin to the relief of Peking. Since it seemed necessary for the army to be under a unified command, the suggestion of the German Emperor that Count Waldersee be made supreme commander was given consideration by the Powers. American acceptance of the idea was discussed in another telephone conversation between the President and the War Department. Secretary Root favored accepting Waldersee as supreme commander provided that the American military units retained their integrity with their own ranking officer in command. To make sure of this he suggested to the President that compliance with the Emperor's offer be hedged with certain conditions and restrictions. The President's attitude is made evident in some passages of his reply. "It seems to me," he said, "that the acceptance of the Emperor's suggestion is not quite as generous as it ought to be. That is, there are so many conditions and qualifications suggested in the note as to make our acceptance of the present offer contingent upon things that may happen in the future. That is all very well, but is it necessary in our reply to the Emperor to do more than to accept with gratification the services tendered?" [13] In answer to Root's apprehension that Waldersee's supreme command would mean surrendering the right of command to a foreign officer, the President replied: "We do not surrender the right, as I view it.

---

[11] Dennett, p. 302.

[12] Olcott, Vol. II, pp. 236–38.

[13] Olcott, Vol. II, p. 248.

We are only agreeing to concurrent action in which, for efficiency and convenience, it is better to have a single head." [14]

On August 14 the allied forces, numbering nearly 20,000 troops, more than one fourth of them Americans, reached Peking, rescued the legations, and occupied the city. At this stage President McKinley, who felt that this success should mark the end of their mission in China, urged the prompt withdrawal of American troops. He was therefore very responsive to a proposal from Russia that American and Russian soldiers be moved out of China so that negotiations by the Powers with the Chinese authorities for the settlement of their claims against China might proceed. Though the Russian proposal was rejected, the President grew more and more insistent. "I know of no way to get out but to come out," he wrote to Hay, who tried in vain to dissuade him from such a course. "I have this general notion that we should get out of Pekin with the least possible delay. Russia is intending to withdraw and we should in accord with our note, even if there is no other reason and I think there are many reasons why we should come out. We want to avoid being in Pekin for a long time and it must be a long time if we stay there for diplomatic negotiations and without our intending it, we may be drawn into currents that would be unfortunate." [15] To the Secretary's dismay a reduction of American troops in China was ordered by the President, and by the end of 1900 less than two fifths of them remained.

By that time the Powers had presented a joint note to the Chinese containing their demands on China, including indemnities for losses suffered from the Boxer disorder. During the negotiations the United States was successful in prevailing on them to be moderate in their demands and to scale down their claims for indemnity. The total amount, approximately $333,-000,000, was thought not to have been excessive. Of this sum the

---

[14] Olcott, Vol. II, p. 250.

[15] Dennett, pp. 314–15. In a dispatch to Washington, General Chaffee, in command of the American contingent, stated that he and other officers were agreed that, unless the troops were removed, conditions in China would grow worse (Dawes, *Journal,* p. 248).

share awarded to the United States, $25,000,000 was found on later investigation to have exceeded American losses by $14,-000,000.[16] Negotiations were concluded on September 7, 1901, on which date the signing of the Boxer Protocol took place.

---

[16] Dennett, p. 316; Latané, p. 112.

CHAPTER XIX

The Verdict on Imperialism

As President McKinley drew near the end of his first term the stock argument for his re-election was that the country did not want a change. It was satisfied to let well enough alone. Four years before, the Republicans had been elected to office in response to a powerful demand for a change of administration, under a pledge to restore prosperity. Rarely, it seemed, had an administration had a better claim to be continued in power on the strength of its past performance. The country basked in the warm light of a prosperity shared alike by its businessmen, merchants, farmers, and wage-earners. Speaking before the Ohio Republican State Convention in April, 1900, Mark Hanna declared that since the Republicans had fulfilled all that they had promised in 1896, they could stand fearlessly on their record.[1]

When the Republican National Convention met at Philadelphia, harmony and understanding prevailed. Although the

[1] Croly, p. 303.

President had remained silent on the question of his renomination, it was generally assumed that he would be renominated. The party bosses, Platt, Quay, and others, were there, to be sure, but not for the purpose of bargaining for the nomination of a favorite son. As for campaign issues, the McKinley administration's record of achievements was thought to be so impressive that the platform was mainly a recital of its successes. But in view of the tremendous consolidations in recent years among railroads and industrial corporations, a resolution on the subject of trusts, written by Hanna, was included by the Committee on Resolutions.

Although great aggregations of capital were deemed necessary to promote foreign markets and trade, the resolution condemned, in the words of the Sherman Anti-Trust Act of 1890, conspiracies and combinations that restrained trade and it favored legislation to curb them. Republican voters, enjoying prosperity after so many lean years, were not likely to be for such a declaration by their party.[2] They were quite willing to accept the trusts as more or less a part of the country's economic development. Those who attacked these benevolent enterprises because of their very bigness were, after all, prophets of gloom and foes of prosperity.

Since the Democratic Convention, to meet in July, would denounce the McKinley administration for plunging the country into a huge imperialistic venture, that issue could not be evaded. The administration's policy of overseas expansion, though popular, particularly in the Middle West, might become extremely embarrassing if the insurrection in the Philippines dragged on at a great cost in life and treasure. Moreover, competition of Philippine tobacco and sugar with their own products was something that American tobacco and sugar growers were not likely to accept complacently. The President's wish that the Philippines be not too much stressed was therefore complied with by the Republican platform-makers when they asserted that acquisition of these remote islands by the United States followed as a

---

[2] Croly, pp. 206–7.

necessary result of their conquest. Now that they were American possessions, the Republican platform promised to exploit the opportunity for trade in the Orient and the Open Door in China by building a merchant marine.[3]

The Republican National Convention of 1900 was memorable for the extraordinary interest shown in the question of McKinley's running mate. But for that the delegates, after transacting the cut-and-dried business of renominating McKinley and adopting a platform, might as well have adjourned on the third day and gone home. But the nomination of a Vice-President, ordinarily a routine matter, was of transcendent importance at the Philadelphia convention, and the delegates were as much keyed up over the second place on the ticket as they ordinarily were over the first. Had Vice-President Hobart lived, he would doubtless have been renominated. In the circumstances the problem of finding a successor who would strengthen the ticket was given careful consideration by the party leaders, particularly Mark Hanna, who again acted as McKinley's campaign manager. The President, though repeatedly urged to make known his preference, refused to do so. It would probably have been Secretary of the Navy Long, Senator Allison of Iowa, or former Secretary of the Interior Bliss. But, since none of these was available, the field was narrowed down to Governor Roosevelt of New York, Jonathan Dolliver, Congressman from Iowa, Timothy Woodruff of New York, and Senator Fairbanks of Indiana.[4]

The most prominent of this group was Roosevelt. His popularity as a war hero and as governor of his state had reached a peak. Against Hanna's wishes and perhaps the President's as well, the former commander of the Rough Riders was being

---

[3] Other resolutions were those approving annexation of Hawaii, commending participation of the United States in the Hague Peace Conference, asserting steadfast adherence to the Monroe Doctrine, and declaring that the pledge to Cuba had been fully kept (Latané, p. 127).

[4] Croly, pp. 308–9. According to Stoddard, McKinley was unmoved by every appeal from Hanna and others to express a preference. At length he authorized his secretary, George B. Cortelyou, to make it known that the administration did not want its friends to commit it to any candidate other than the one chosen by the convention (*As I Knew Them,* p. 249).

pushed for the Vice-Presidency by Senator Platt of New York. Platt's preference for Roosevelt was entirely ignoble. It stemmed from a personal dislike of him and a determination to prevent his renomination for the governorship; for as governor Roosevelt had acted in complete indifference to the will of the Platt political machine. There had also been frequent clashes over matters of policy between him and Platt, and they enhanced the Senator's deep resentment. What better way of getting rid of this young and ambitious upstart than to have him laid up on that ideally dusty shelf for aspiring politicians, the Vice-Presidency? It was a scheme equal in craftiness to any that had ever emanated from the fertile brain of New York's top politician. And it was abetted by Senator Quay, boss of the Republican machine in Pennsylvania, who also had an ax to grind.[5]

What was Roosevelt's response to the Platt-Quay scheme? The story as told by him and quoted by Hanna's biographer, Croly, was that he refused pointblank to be railroaded out of the governor's office into the Vice-Presidency; that if they persisted in their scheme he would go before the Convention and expose their designs. At a meeting of the New York delegates for the purpose of nominating him for Vice-President Roosevelt announced that he would not accept the nomination and would come out at once as a candidate for re-election to succeed himself as governor.[6]

Doubtless the Platt-Quay scheme would have failed had not an irresistible demand from western state delegations swept the convention. The Westerners meant to put over their favorite, despite all opposition. They would not accept a refusal from the candidate himself. Evidently staggered by this demonstration of his popularity, Roosevelt gave the delegates the cue they wanted. On June 21, after McKinley's renomination by unanimous

---

[5] Quay's enmity was not necessarily against Roosevelt; it was against Senator Hanna, who feared and disliked Roosevelt. Hanna had made a bitter foe of Quay when on April 24, 1900, he had cast the deciding vote in favor of the report of the Committee on Privileges and Elections, thereby preventing the Pennsylvania Senator from taking his seat (Croly, p. 283).

[6] Croly, pp. 311 ff.

vote, the colonel's name was placed before the convention, and he received the votes of all but one delegate.[7]

To Hanna, Roosevelt's nomination was gall. He had come to the Convention determined to find a Vice-Presidential candidate who would carry on the McKinley policies. To realize his purpose he thought of trying to stop the stampede for Roosevelt by opposing it on the floor. But friends of the McKinley administration, in view of the universal preference for "Teddy," feared the unpopularity of such opposition. Even on the day before Roosevelt's nomination Hanna hoped, by organizing his forces, to block the Governor's candidacy. But at that point Charles G. Dawes, friendly to both McKinley and Hanna, intervened. In a long-distance telephone conversation with the President Dawes was instructed by McKinley to urge Hanna to abandon further efforts to stop Roosevelt. The energetic campaign manager reluctantly complied. In a statement to the Convention Hanna advised the delegates to make the Roosevelt nomination unanimous along with McKinley's.[8]

The young New Yorker, it will be noted, was in no sense a disinterested spectator of the exciting contest that culminated in his nomination. He had expressed himself both in public and in private as emphatically opposed, alleging his desire to continue in the governor's chair in Albany and to pursue to successful conclusion some policies in which he heartily believed. In spite of such repeated protestations, Roosevelt went to Philadelphia and strode dramatically down the aisle of the convention hall wearing a cowboy sombrero.[9] Other evidences seem to show that as governor he was moved by considerations of personal ambition and self-advancement. He would have given up the governorship to become Secretary of War when Alger was dismissed. To his

---

[7] Croly, pp. 314–17. It was the opinion of this writer that Roosevelt's nomination greatly strengthened the Republican ticket, for he was the outstanding hero of the Cuban War. Both McKinley and Hanna, in stressing national prosperity as the chief end of the Republican Party, overlooked the popularity of the war, particularly in the West, where the demand for Roosevelt's nomination was centered.

[8] Oberholtzer, p. 632.

[9] Oberholtzer, p. 630.

disappointment, Elihu Root was appointed. Again, he had his eye on that office when it was expected that Root would be a candidate for Vice-President. He fondly hoped, too, that he would be selected as the first civil governor of the Philippines. In corresponding with his friend Senator Lodge in July, 1899, Roosevelt frankly stated that he would welcome nomination to the Vice-Presidency.[10]

There was a somber undertone, too, in this dramatic contest—a mysterious hint of some tragic dénouement in the not distant future. "Don't you know," Hanna asked Timothy Woodruff, who keenly aspired to be named with McKinley on the Republican ticket, "that there is only one life between the Presidency and the Vice-Presidency and that it would be foolish to nominate a man for Vice-President who was not big enough to be President?"[11] In dismay at the tumultuous efforts of Roosevelt's admirers to effect his nomination Hanna cried out to his friends: "Don't you understand that there is just one life between this crazy man and the Presidency?"[12] Could he have had in mind the possibility that McKinley might not live to complete another term? It was rumored in the spring of 1900 that specialists at the University of Pennsylvania whom McKinley had gone to consult discovered that he was suffering from an advanced stage of Bright's disease. This knowledge must have reached the politicians; it explains the rumor that before his renomination they were frankly though secretly discussing the possibility of his death.[13] "Could any of these rumors of McKinley's ailment have reached Roosevelt, who for a long time vehemently protested that he would not accept the nomination?" is the question raised by a Roosevelt biographer.[14] It is at least an interesting topic for speculation.

10 Oberholtzer, p. 630.

11 Oberholtzer, p. 630*n*.

12 W. F. McCaleb, *Theodore Roosevelt,* p. 99.

13 McCaleb, p. 103.

14 McCaleb, p. 104. In a letter to Henry Adams dated October 21, 1901, John Hay wrote: "I was more surprised to learn from the autopsy of the President that he was dying of old age at 58, if he had not been shot" (McCaleb, *Theodore Roosevelt,* pp. 103–4; all quotations by permission of Albert and Charles Boni, Inc.).

During the early months of 1900 numerous political conventions met and adopted party platforms, but not all of them chose separate standard-bearers. One of the most important, at Washington in February, included the Farmers' Alliance; it pledged itself to support W. J. Bryan on a free-silver issue.[15] The Populists were in a desperately divided state. One wing, opposed to fusion with the Democrats, met at Cincinnati on May 10 and nominated Wharton Barker of Pennsylvania for President and Ignatius Donnelly of Minnesota for Vice-President. The Fusionists, who were ready to join with the Democrats, met on the same day at Sioux Falls, South Dakota. They chose Bryan by acclamation on a radical platform demanding free and unlimited coinage of silver and placing the agencies of the government under direct popular control in lieu of representative control. They also declared themselves opposed to imperialism.[16] Both the Silver Republicans, who convened in Kansas City at the same time as the Democrats, and the Liberty Congress of the American League of Anti-Imperialists, meeting in Indianapolis on August 16, endorsed Bryan. Other organizations to put forth candidates were the Socialist Labor Party, with Eugene Debs as their candidate, the Social Democratic Party, who nominated a man from Massachusetts, Maloney by name, and the United Christian Party.[17] The campaign of 1900 fairly swarmed with party candidates and platforms.

It was said that about all the Democrats at Kansas City needed to do when it came to drafting their platform was to ratify what had already been done by other conventions.

It was, of course, not that simple. The Democrats, in fact, showed much independence in making their party declarations. Imperialism was held to be the "paramount" issue. In the words of the Declaration of Independence, the party took its position on the principle that government rested on the consent of the governed; the new colonial policy was contrary to that principle and inconsistent with American free institutions. In a clear

---

[15] Oberholtzer, p. 635.
[16] Oberholtzer, p. 635; Latané, pp. 124–25.
[17] Latané, p. 130.

and vigorous style the platform denounced Republican policy in the Philippines and demanded an immediate expression from the Republicans of their intention to give the Filipinos stable government and independence. The Democratic declaration on the trust question, in contrast with the evasiveness of the Republicans, was clear-cut and emphatic. The trusts, it stated, were fostered by the Republican Dingley tariff.[18]

The most vulnerable part of the Democratic platform was the money plank. On it the Resolutions Committee was seriously divided. About half of the Committee argued against adopting the free-silver issue that had proved so unfortunate in 1896. But Bryan's contention about the evils of the gold standard still so dominated the thinking of the others that they decided by a close vote to commit the party to an "endorsement of the principles of the National Democratic platform adopted at Chicago in 1896, namely, 'the immediate restoration of the free and unlimited coinage of silver and gold at the ratio 16 to 1, without waiting for the aid or consent of any other nation.'" [19]

The Kansas City convention, except for the delegations from eastern states, was so dominated by Bryanism that Bryan's nomination on a platform dictated by himself was a foregone conclusion. He was nominated by acclamation on the second day, and after an unsuccessful attempt to nominate Richard Croker of New York as Vice-President the delegates turned to the Mid-West and selected A. E. Stephenson of Illinois, who had served as Vice-President under Cleveland.[20] The fact that Bryan was the presidential candidate of both the fusion Populists and the Democrats made it necessary for Democrats and Populists in each state to have a common set of electors.

---

[18] Latané, p. 129.

[19] Latané, pp. 129–30. Dunn is our authority for the story that Bryan practically forced the convention to include the free-silver declaration by threatening to decline the nomination unless it were included. The decision of the Resolutions Committee in favor of the money plank came about when one of its members, a Hawaiian, changed his vote under pressure by Bryan free-silver advocates (Vol. I, pp. 342–43). According to Latané, David Hill of New York, who opposed the silver issue, was kept off the committee, thereby causing it to yield to Bryan's dictation (p. 128).

[20] Oberholtzer, p. 636.

In the opening weeks of the campaign Republican confidence ran high. Most Republicans shared the opinion of *The New York Times* that they would win as in 1896; that the people would make a wise choice between national honor and dishonor, between ruin and safety. But as the campaign progressed there was a change. Businessmen grew apprehensive at the thought of Democratic success and the possibility that the single-gold-standard dollar might be replaced by Bryan's double standard. Business could not prosper in this state of mind, and a slowing-down set in during the summer and fall, with much unemployment. Concerned lest McKinley lose votes to Bryan, Mark Hanna appealed to the industrialists to keep workmen at their jobs until business picked up. By personal intervention he succeeded in ending a serious strike of anthracite coal miners in Pennsylvania, which had threatened the loss of many votes in a normally Republican state.[21] On the eve of the election friends of the administration were fearful of the outcome.[22] Roosevelt's apprehension was strikingly revealed in conversation with a friend. "The combination of all the lunatics, all the idiots, all the knaves, all the cowards, and all the honest people who are hopelessly slow-witted is a formidable one to overcome when backed by the Solid South. This is the combination we have to face."[23] In the midst of this gloom came an unusual offer of help from one of the opposing candidates—a suggestion by the presidential candidate of the anti-fusion wing of the Populists, made in a strictly confidential letter to President McKinley. The Populists, the letter stated, would try to split the Democratic Party of the South in a campaign to win from Bryan the electoral votes of Georgia, and probably those of Texas and Alabama. The Pop-

---

[21] Croly, p. 328.

[22] In a letter of October 31 John Hay wrote: "This last week is getting on everybody's nerves. I do not believe defeat to be possible, though it is evident that this last month of Bryan roaring out his desperate appeals to hate and envy, is having its effect on the dangerous classes." On the same day he wrote to Henry Adams: "Our folks are curiously nervous about next Tuesday. The canvass is all right, the betting also. But nobody knows what Jack Cade may do" (Thayer).

[23] McCaleb, p. 101.

ulist candidate accompanied his proposal with an appeal for
money from the Republican campaign chest to carry on a more
aggressive campaign in those states.[24]

The foremost issues of the campaign were imperialism and
the money standard, with the first paramount. It was the major
theme discussed by Democratic and Republican speakers, particularly Roosevelt and Bryan, who vied with one another in dis-
tances traveled, cities visited, and audiences addressed. On a
tour through the Northwest as far as the Rocky Mountains the
"American cyclone," as Buffalo Bill called Roosevelt, spoke for
American world power and the duty the United States must
assume as a world force. Taunting his anti-imperialist opponents
as cowards, he reminded them: "We are a nation of men, not a
nation of weaklings. The American people," he shouted, "were
as ready to face their responsibilities in the Orient as they were
ready to face them at home." [25] The acquisition of new territories, Roosevelt declared, belonged to American national expansion, and expansion was not imperialism or militarism.[26]

For the second time as a Presidential candidate Bryan demonstrated his skill and endurance as a campaigner. The essential
weakness in the Democratic armor lay in the fact that, no matter
how much they might deplore the acquisition of Porto Rico and
the Philippines, the United States, now that it had them, faced
the task of administering them properly. It was against the Republican policy in this respect that Bryan directed his attack.
Why, he would ask, should not the Filipinos, like the Cubans,
be free and independent? If elected, what would he do with the
Philippines? He would call Congress in special session soon
after his inauguration and recommend that it provide a stable
form of government in the Philippines—that it grant them independence as it proposed to do for Cuba. Finally, he would have
Congress extend over them the protecting shield of the Monroe
Doctrine, to safeguard them from external interference.[27] Such

---

[24] Oberholtzer, Vol. V, p. 639.
[25] McCaleb, p. 101.
[26] Rhodes, pp. 141–42.
[27] Rhodes, p. 137.

a policy, Bryan declared, would free the United States from the charge of forcing an unwilling people to accept a rule imposed by a long, bloody war of conquest.

McKinley was not active in the campaign. He remained in Washington much of the time, occasionally going to Canton, but not to receive and address visiting delegations as in 1896. He did not deem it necessary to campaign. "Four years ago," he explained, "I was a private citizen and the candidate of my party for President. It was my privilege to aid in bringing success to my party by making a campaign. Now I am President of the whole people, and while I am a candidate again, I feel that the proprieties demand that the President should refrain making a political canvass in his own behalf." [28] McKinley's most important utterance was his letter of acceptance of July 12. About two thirds of it had to do with the Philippines. "The Philippines are ours," he stated, "and American authority must be supreme throughout the archipelago. . . . There must be no scuttle policy. There will be no turning aside, no wavering, no retreat. No blow has been struck except for liberty and humanity and none will be. We will perform without fear, every national and international obligation. The Republican Party . . . broke the shackles of 4,000,000 slaves and made them free and to the party of Lincoln has come another supreme opportunity which it has bravely met in the liberation of 10,000,000 of the human family from the yoke of imperialism." [29]

Mark Hanna's active stumping made the campaign of 1900 quite different from the one four years before. Outside of Ohio he was unknown as a speaker, and for that reason he refrained for a time from speaking. But pressure from Republican state committees in the West and Northwest persuaded him to make an extended tour through the strong Bryan states west of the Mississippi. He was especially desirous of carrying the fight into Bryan's Nebraska and into South Dakota, from which hailed the free-silver Senator Pettigrew, a personal enemy of Hanna. Some

---

[28] Dunn, *From Harding to Harrison*, Vol. I, pp. 347–48 (quoted by permission of G. P. Putnam's Sons).

[29] Olcott, Vol. II, p. 287.

of his friends, fearing that the trip might do more harm than good, advised against it. The President apparently shared this belief: he authorized his Postmaster General to go to Chicago to dissuade Hanna. The messenger only succeeded in ruffling Hanna's temper and making him more determined to go through with the tour as planned.[30]

It turned out to be a big success. Immense crowds greeted the Republican campaign manager wherever he was scheduled to speak and listened to him with much interest. His chief object was to impress on his hearers that they owed their prosperity to the McKinley administration and to urge them to vote for its continuance in power. At Lincoln, Bryan's home town, Hanna directed a vigorous counterattack against the charge of the Democratic candidate that Hanna had raised a large fund to intimidate laboring men, bribe election officers, and buy votes. He would hurl Bryan's words back in his teeth as a rank falsehood.[31] At the Chicago stockyards, where Hanna appeared to address a group of workmen, he was met by a hostile crowd determined to prevent him from speaking; it raised so much disturbance that he could not be heard. By keeping a cool head and waiting for the tumult to subside he gained the crowd's attention and delivered a remarkable speech.[32]

Above all, Hanna's public appearance helped to reveal to the people the man's true personality. He had been grossly misrepresented by his enemies. The press delighted in publishing cartoons depicting him as an inhuman monster.[33] Thousands before whom he appeared saw, instead of a bloated millionaire covered over with dollar signs, a man of simple democratic bearing who spoke a language they knew and whose thoughts they easily comprehended. They were struck primarily by his honesty and sincerity. To quote from Hanna's biographer: "He was not separated from them by differences of standards and tastes or by an

---

[30] Croly, pp. 332–33.

[31] Croly, p. 338.

[32] Rhodes, p. 141.

[33] At Winside, Nebraska, an enormous placard bore these words of warning: "Populist Farmers Beware. Chain Your Children to Yourselves or Put Them Under the Bed. Mark Hanna Is in Town." (Croly, p. 338.)

intellectual or professional sophistication. The roughness of much of his public speaking and its lack of form . . . were an essential part of its actual success. He stamped himself on his speeches just as he stamped himself on his business. His audiences had to pass judgment on the man more than on the message and the man could not but look good to them." [34]

The Democrats carried the message of anti-imperialism into the Middle West and the eastern states. They concentrated attention on the wrongful use of the armed forces in the Philippines to subjugate a race that longed to be free and politically independent. This example of imperialism and militarism, they contended, transcended every issue. Compared with it, the money question was of minor consequence. For gold was, after all, the legally defined standard, and nothing, not even Bryan's election, could change it. On the other hand, imperialism and militarism would destroy the Republic, would undermine its foundations. This emphasis was one way of escaping the embarrassing dilemma caused by Bryan's insistence on free silver as an issue in the Democratic platform.[35]

Hanna's Republican campaign program in 1900 was much like that of 1896. McKinley emblems and buttons were issued again. There was a vast outpouring of campaign literature. The country was deluged with posters, pamphlets, and leaflets, many of them in foreign languages. The total campaign fund rose to about $2,500,000, not all of which was used. As before, the money came almost entirely from business firms, particularly the corporations, which had grown in size and number. Combination and reorganization of American business enterprise on a large scale had gone forward in nearly every industry, the state anti-trust laws and the Sherman Anti-Trust Act notwithstanding.[36] Because many large corporations had come into existence without regard to those laws and grown in defiance of them, corporations, pop-

[34] Croly, p. 340.

[35] Oberholtzer, p. 641.

[36] Trusts and holding companies were being formed from smaller independent units by promoters and underwriters such as J. P. Morgan & Company, who promoted the United States Steel Corporation and others (Peck, pp. 633–34).

ularly labeled trusts, had become more and more the objects
of public suspicion and political attack. By 1900 they had come
to realize their dependence on the government, and more particularly on the political party that promised them protection.
To the Republican Party, as the one interested in big business
and the furtherance of its prosperity, the corporations therefore
turned and readily paid the assessments levied on them by the
campaign managers. The point to be remembered, however, and
the one the corporations apparently overlooked, was that their
contributions would be regarded by the public pretty much as
premium payments for protection or insurance against prosecu-
tion by the government under the anti-trust law. By their contributions they were exposing themselves even more to public cen-
sure. In both 1896 and 1900 there was a strikingly close associa-
tion of the corporations with the Republicans as the party of the
business interests, and they opened their purses liberally in its
interest.

Anti-imperialism was stressed more in New England and the
eastern states by the Democrats than elsewhere, for it carried
more weight in those sections. This fact was probably one reason
why Bryan gained more votes in the East in 1900 than four years
before. Another reason may have been that many Democrats
in those states who, from fear of Bryan's free-silver crusade, had
voted against him in 1896 did not regard the issue so seriously
in 1900. His gain in popular votes, however, was not enough to
have much effect on the electoral vote.

Neither anti-imperialism nor free silver met with much popular response in the West. Many western Republicans who had
voted for free silver and the Democratic ticket in 1896 apparently did not look upon the silver question as of such importance
and returned to the Republican fold in 1900. They helped
McKinley carry seven western states that had gone to Bryan
four years before.[37] Among Bryan's political bedfellows in 1900
were such strange opposites as Richard Croker, head of Tam-
many Hall, and Carl Schurz, who led the anti-imperialists. Bryan

---

[37] Olcott, Vol. II, p. 292; Dunn, Vol. I, pp. 348–49.

At White House receptions Mrs. McKinley would occupy a chair beside the President as he stood in the receiving line, so that he might give her instant attention if necessary.[8] Accustomed to treat his wife with every courtesy, the President must have been annoyed by the social formalities at Washington. A friend who had dinner with the McKinleys at the White House soon after the first inauguration told an interesting incident: The company being seated, the butler came in to serve the meal. He went first to the President and served him before going to the others. After he had gone the President remarked: "This is one of the things I cannot get used to. All my married life, Mrs. McKinley has been served first, but it is a custom and we cannot change it. We are governed by White House etiquette handed down for generations."[9] He did, however, disregard the custom by which the President at official dinners was expected to sit at one end of the table and the First Lady at the opposite end. On such occasions she always sat at his right.[10]

Their marriage was a beautiful union; they were inseparably bound by mystic cords of love and romance. No better proof could be offered than the incidents recounted by McKinley's biographer. Summoned from Washington by news of his wife's critical illness, the young Congressman was told by the attending doctor that there was no hope. He had tried in vain to revive her after she had been unconscious for many hours. When the doctor was gone McKinley began a long, desperate battle to bring his wife back to consciousness. Through the night, for hours he labored over the still form, chafing and caressing her hands and face. Night faded into dawn and he was still struggling to save his loved one from the clutch of death. At long last she gave signs of reviving. She moved slightly, opened her eyes, and tightened her hold on his hand. "I knew you would come," she whispered, and fell into a sweet, natural sleep.[11]

Another episode recounted by the same author sounds like

---

[8] Dunn, Vol. II, p. 363.
[9] Kohlsaat, p. 63.
[10] Prindiville, p. 193.
[11] Olcott, Vol. II, pp. 362–63.

a tale of chivalry in the days of knighthood. While McKinley was governor of Ohio he and his wife lived in the Neill House, directly facing the Capitol grounds. Each morning on the way to the office he would turn before entering the building and doff his hat to the wife watching at her window. In the afternoon, always at exactly the same hour, he would excuse himself, step to the window, and gallantly wave his handkerchief to Mrs. McKinley, who would return the salutation from the window of her room.[12]

During their years in the White House the McKinleys were active in the social life of the capital. They entertained extensively, and their guests included public officials, friends and acquaintances, and members of the McKinley and Saxton families. Very illuminating on the social activities of the McKinley régime is the *Journal* of Charles G. Dawes. His daily entries during the McKinley years tell of many pleasant evenings enjoyed by Dawes and his wife at the White House. They tell of theater parties in which the Daweses were included as guests and of numerous business and pleasure trips on which they accompanied the President and Mrs. McKinley, members of the Cabinet, and other dignitaries.[13] As guests of the McKinleys the Daweses spent many an informal evening at the White House playing cards, the favorite game being euchre, which was much enjoyed by both the President and his wife. At other times the evening's entertainment included performances by celebrated artists who happened to be in Washington for scheduled appearances. Dawes and his wife were much impressed by a recital

---

[12] Olcott, Vol. II, pp. 361–62.

[13] Dawes came to know McKinley as governor of Ohio and as presidential candidate in 1896. He was strongly attracted to him and devoted much time and effort to working for McKinley's nomination. Dawes was instrumental in securing the election by the Illinois Republican State Convention of delegates pledged to support McKinley for President at the Republican National Convention. During the campaign of 1896 Dawes was made one of the nine members of the Executive Committee of the Republican National Committee. As such he was responsible to Hanna, McKinley's manager, for the raising and disbursing of large sums of campaign funds. After his election McKinley appointed Dawes Comptroller of the Currency. Dawes and his wife grew to be on very intimate terms with the McKinleys.

by the cellist Stern and a violin recital by a seven-year-old boy prodigy. On warm summer evenings the McKinleys and their guests would sit on the rear White House portico and listen to the Marine band. Theater parties, which usually included Mrs. McKinley but not the President, provided much diversion, and it was not unusual for theatergoers at the Lafayette Square Opera House and the Columbian Theater to see guests and friends with Mrs. McKinley occupying box seats at plays in which some of the great actors of the day performed—Henry Irving, Joe Jefferson, Julia Marlowe. Every year on the day after Easter, as the Dawes diary records, large crowds came to witness the popular egg-rolling on the White House lawn, at which the McKinleys were usually interested spectators.

An air of pleasing informality prevailed when friends came to see them. Of a Sunday evening the singing of familiar songs and hymns was a favorite pastime. There was much levity on occasions when a Cabinet member would lay aside his official dignity for a moment to give an exhibition of skill or lack of skill as a vocalist or as a dancer of the Virginia reel. After the guests had gone the President found delight in chatting and smoking with a few intimates. These learned to know and understand him as most persons never did.[14]

From the Dawes diary we learn, too, that the President and Mrs. McKinley were fond of taking drives together. The mistress of the White House was not permitted to drive unaccompanied. The President seems to have got much relaxation from the cares of office by taking regular drives with his wife. But there were times when such trips were made chiefly for her benefit rather than for his own. Prominent officials and advisers of the President often went driving with him to talk over matters of state, and doubtless decisions affecting weighty matters of public policy were made on such excursions.

The pleasure that the McKinleys found in visits to their old home in Canton is made clear in the diary. At Canton lived most of the McKinleys and the Saxtons, besides a host of old friends

---

[14] Olcott,Vol. II, pp. 365 ff.

and neighbors. Near by was the McKinley farm, often visited by
the Presidential couple. It was their favorite place for a vacation,
an ideal spot for rest and relaxation, though occasionally the
scene of important public transactions; e.g., the formal notifica-
tion of McKinley's nomination in 1896 and again in 1900.

During their time in the White House, the McKinleys did
much traveling, some of it for pleasure and some on official business. The diary speaks of two trips to the South, both primarily
for pleasure, on which the Daweses were guests in a section of
the President's private car. On the first, in June 1897, the President and his wife visited Hot Springs, Virginia, then crossed into
Tennessee to Nashville and Chattanooga, where they were shown
over celebrated battlefields of the Civil War.[15] On the second
trip, in May 1899, the Presidential party took drives from Hot
Springs to Warm Springs to view a famous exhibit of historical
relics, and to other near-by points of interest. After an enjoyable
fortnight in that renowned portion of the Old Dominion they returned to Washington in the same special train.[16]

There was, of course, much purely official and political traveling to be done. It appears from the Dawes diary that Mrs.
McKinley generally accompanied her husband on such trips. On
one of them, in April 1897, the President went to New York to
attend the dedication ceremony at General Grant's tomb. He put
in five strenuous days. After reviewing a procession of sixty
thousand Civil War veterans, the Chief Executive delivered the
main address of the occasion and, with Vice-President Hobart,
attended a public reception at the Union League Club.[17] Another
official trip was to Chicago in October, 1899. A mere recital of
the events recorded in the diary suggests the strenuousness of
the Presidential schedule. McKinley officiated at the laying of the
cornerstone of a new Federal building, spoke as the guest of
honor at a banquet, went to a luncheon given him by the Union
League Club, attended a banquet at the auditorium at which he
delivered an important address, and was present at another ban-

---

[15] Dawes, pp. 122–23.
[16] Dawes, pp. 191–92.
[17] Dawes, pp. 118–19.

quet in his honor by the Commercial Club, where he spoke to a group of Union workers. Dawes noted that Mrs. McKinley held up well during most of the trip, but had to retire part of the time to her hotel room for rest and seclusion.[18]

On April 29, 1901, following his second inauguration, the President set out on an extensive speaking tour through the South and West. The trip was carefully planned, and he took with him notes for speeches on tariff reciprocity and control of the trusts. These were to be paramount issues of his second term. On board the Presidential train when it pulled out of Washington were the McKinleys, members of the Cabinet and their wives, and invited guests besides a large staff of newspapermen. "Of all the trips made by McKinley during his Presidency," wrote Olcott, "this last one aroused more genuine interest throughout the country, yet possessed less political significance than any of the others. It was a continuous demonstration of the firm hold which the President had gained upon the affections of the people." [19] His journey through the South seemed to crown with success the efforts he had made two years before to draw the two great sections of the country together. At each leading Southern city, Memphis, New Orleans, Houston, San Antonio, and El Paso, the President was tendered ovations by the crowds that gathered to see and hear him.

At El Paso Mrs. McKinley became ill, and she grew worse as they proceeded. When the train reached the Pacific coast all further engagements were canceled, and Mrs. McKinley was taken to San Francisco for treatment and rest. On May 15, according to Dawes, the newspapers carried alarming reports of her illness, and at Washington her condition was thought to be so critical that it was feared she might not recover.[20] For two weeks the President remained in San Francisco, almost constantly at his wife's bedside. Secretary Hay meanwhile acted as

---

[18] Dawes, pp. 202–3. The *Journal* tells of traveling by Mrs. McKinley on trips to Baltimore with her nieces, and to New York, once with Mrs. Dawes and once with Mrs. Dawes and her husband (pp. 148, 176, 254).

[19] Olcott, Vol. II, pp. 300–302.

[20] Dawes, p. 267.

head of the Presidential party.[21] The return to Washington was made as soon as possible and with the utmost speed. Mrs. McKinley did not leave the capital again until midsummer, when she and the President went to Canton for the rest of the summer.[22]

During her illness the nation's sympathy was once more centered in the First Lady. People scanned the newspapers for the latest reports on her condition. When she was reported as out of danger and convalescing, the people were relieved and grateful for her sake and for the sake of her devoted husband. Their hearts were touched as they remembered the many times when as Congressman, as governor, and more recently as the nation's Chief Executive McKinley had always given her unselfishly of his time and strength, often at the risk of his own health.

Long years of patient, unremitting devotion to an invalid wife were certain to take a toll, and early. McKinley's friends fancied that they saw a change in him while he was still a young man. He became, in the words of one of Hanna's biographers, "a soft-spoken, watchful nurse in his own house and a worried guest if he was in company without his charge. He ascended," this writer continued, "into the headlines of the newspapers with this burden and it was genuine, wasting his time, hurting his health and wearying his friends so that they canonized him before he was forty years old." [23] Could this same thought have been in Hanna's mind when, in speaking of the President's admirable qualities as a husband, he exclaimed: "McKinley is a saint"? [24]

21 Olcott, Vol. II, pp. 303–4.
22 Dawes, p. 274.
23 Beer, p. 103 (quoted by permission of Alfred A. Knopf).
24 Rhodes, p. 10.

CHAPTER XXI

The Emerging Statesman

More than thirty years after McKinley had left the scene he was described by one of John Hay's biographers as "one of the most obscure major figures in American history."[1] It is perhaps as master politician that McKinley had been known and judged—the ideal politician, in whom, to quote from an outstanding journalist, "our politics reached its finest flower."[2] Certainly McKinley was at home when dealing with politicians. He had the ability, as Elihu Root once remarked, "to understand their thoughts . . . to understand what they want, to get on with them. Hoover didn't, Taft didn't, but McKinley did to perfection."[3] Granted, then, that McKinley was an exceptionally able politician, is he in any sense to be rated superior to such mediocre Presidents as Taylor, Fillmore, Pierce, Buchanan, and Harding, all of them skilled, no doubt, in the art of politics, but generally considered to have merited the obscurity to which they have been relegated?

Examination of his letters and private papers for a clue to

[1] Dennett, p. 207.
[2] W. A. White, *Masks in a Pageant*, p. 166.
[3] Jessup, Vol. II, p. 142.

his place in history is not likely to be rewarding. McKinley did not leave many letters, and those that are accessible are not of much value to the biographer, for it was with the biographer and posterity consciously in mind that he wrote most of them, particularly those of his Presidency.[4]

To many of his contemporaries McKinley no doubt really looked the part of a statesman. They were impressed by his fine appearance, his personal charm, an ever-present air of self-mastery, the frock-coated flawless dignity. But to others these seemingly statesmanlike qualities suggested not a statesman but a politician of rather weak character, easily dominated by stronger, superior advisers. What apparently eluded the attention of most persons who saw and knew McKinley was the expression of his face. The dark, luminous eyes, heavy eyebrows, and Websterian forehead seemed so to mask the inner man that few were permitted to peer inside the mask. John Hay was probably one of the few. McKinley's face reminded Hay of "a genuine Italian ecclesiastical face of the fifteenth century." [5]

He wore the set official expression that features acquire after many years in public life, and it enameled him more thickly as he aged. McKinley's career, it has been pointed out, was like the role of an actor who, before going onstage, has withdrawn and carefully rehearsed his part with the public audience constantly in mind. McKinley, while performing before this audience, took such care not to give offense that his private life and character were obscured under a political cloak of self-restraint and caution.[6]

He attained the peak of his responsibility as President in the years 1898–1901. In the spring of 1898, as we have noted, the nation was gripped by an unparalleled war hysteria. An angry Congress was badgering the President with demands for an explanation of his policy of an amicable settlement of the Cuban

---

[4] Croly, pp. 156, 330–31; White, pp. 173–74.

[5] Dennett, p. 178. "His face was cast in a classic mold; you see faces like it in antique marble in the galleries of the Vatican and in the portraits of the great cardinal-statesmen of Italy" (*Memorial Address,* delivered by Hay before Congress, February 27, 1902).

[6] Dennett, p. 178.

problem. Republican leaders in Congress threatened, unless he complied, to force his hand by pushing through resolutions calling for armed intervention, which meant war.

Until early April McKinley firmly held his ground against the war party and shouldered full responsibility for his Cuban peace policy. Thus far he had displayed the leadership and courage of a statesman. But on April 11 he threw over his peace policy and in a message to Congress recommended forcible intervention, or war. For having thus yielded to the war party, McKinley was accused of weakness. Had he held to his course, as many urged and hoped that he would, and had he succeeded in winning independence for Cuba without war, the statesman would have triumphed over the politicians. This indeed would have been statesmanship of a high order. But if he had failed and the country had gone to war in spite of his efforts to avoid war, and he had been discredited before the nation as commander-in-chief of its armed forces, would McKinley then have been rated a statesman?

A somewhat parallel case had occurred a century before McKinley's time. In 1798 President John Adams showed statesmanship by keeping his country at peace with France, then under the corrupt Directory. America was in the throes of a war frenzy. A militant wing of the Federalist President's divided party dominated Congress. They seized the opportunity to force Adams into war if possible, by voting for warships and for measures of military defense. They authorized the raising of an army of ten thousand volunteers and commissioned Washington's former military aide, Alexander Hamilton, to lead the armed forces. But Adams preferred peace, unpopular though it was, to an unnecessary war that might have been tragic in its consequences to the young American Republic. In his late years Adams was reported to have chosen these words for his epitaph: "Here lies John Adams, who was responsible for keeping peace with France in 1800." It should be added, however, that in 1800 it was not with the French Directory, but with the Consulate Government under Napoleon, that he kept the peace; and Napoleon, like Adams, wanted the two countries to avoid a quarrel.

The end of hostilities with Spain threw more responsibilities on McKinley. Defeat meant Spain's loss of Cuba and Porto Rico and her elimination from the Western Hemisphere. Would it necessarily mean loss of the Philippines and Spain's elimination from the Eastern Hemisphere as well? True, American expansion over the Pacific seemed like manifest destiny. First Alaska, then the Samoan islands, then Hawaii. To carry the Stars and Stripes across to the Philippines and plant them on those faraway islands would launch the United States upon a career of imperialism from which there could be no turning back. Here was an inevasible challenge to America's statesmen.

That the President had at first any thought of annexing new territory, and especially the Philippines, seems very improbable; for McKinley was not naturally imperialistic. But after war was declared he was soon swept along by the current of events that set in with Dewey's signal victory at Manila Bay. A revealing memorandum of McKinley's declared: "While we are conducting war, we must keep all we get; when the war is over, we must keep what we want." [7] The President's intention of annexing territory won from Spain is here clearly made evident. Under the Teller Amendment Cuba, when freed from Spanish rule, would be made independent. But we would keep what we wanted of whatever other spoils might fall into our hands.

The problem was relatively simple so far as Porto Rico was concerned. After deciding that we wanted to annex the island we could demand its surrender as indemnity on the basis of military conquest and occupation. When it came to the Philippines the situation was more complex. Not one of the more than seven thousand islands was conquered and occupied by American arms when the war ended. That would not matter if we wanted to let Spain keep them rather than keep them ourselves. But did we want to set them free from Spanish rule and give them their independence, or did we want to keep all of them, or did we want to keep some and hand the rest back to Spain?

On at least one point the President had made up his mind

---

[7] Millis, p. 175.

before the war was over: he would not consent to their return
to Spain. Resting his claim on the occupation of Manila by
American troops when the protocol went into effect, he first
insisted that the island of Luzon be ceded to the United States
in full sovereign right. McKinley's later determination to demand
all of the Philippines took shape after consultation with leading
Republicans and Democrats, some of whom were for it and
others against. Then followed the President's speaking tour to
the Exposition of Omaha and to peace jubilees in the West and
South, while the peace commission was meeting in Paris. As he
spoke he was deftly sounding public opinion about the Philippines. Were the people interested in seeing the American flag
floating over distant shores? Did they favor keeping the flag
flying over territories where American soldiers had fought, territories that they had taken by valor and now occupied? From the
spontaneous response of the crowds that heard him speak McKinley knew that the people were strongly for territorial expansion,
strongly for keeping the Philippines. Knowing that, he was not
long in making up his mind as to the course he would follow.[8]

The President's trip was a kind of pre-election swing-around-
the-circle campaign. Candidates for seats in Congress were out-
spoken expansionists; so were many Republican newspapers, as
well as party leaders like Lodge and Roosevelt, who were working hard to bring the President to their position.[9] On the other
hand, some of his Cabinet, like Secretary of the Interior Bliss,
tried without success to turn him from his course.[10] McKinley
later stated his own reason for deciding to keep the Philippines;
he stated it to representatives of the Methodist Episcopal Church
whom he was receiving at the White House. He did not want
the Philippines, he told them. But what was he to do with them?
He had taken counsel with leading men of both major parties,
but they could not give him much help. The problem weighed
on his mind, and he walked the floor night after night wrestling

[8] Dunn,Vol. I, p. 279. See also speech made in Savannah, December 17,
1898 (*Speeches and Addresses of McKinley, 1897 to 1900*, pp. 174–75).

[9] Oberholtzer, p. 575.

[10] Millis, p. 383.

with it. Then one night, in answer to a prayer to Almighty God for guidance, it was given him to see that "there was nothing left to do but to take them all and to educate the Filipinos and uplift and Christianize them and by God's grace to do the very best we could by them as our fellowmen for whom Christ also died." [11]

Everything taken into account, McKinley's decision to retain the Philippines was doubtless the best solution. Their return to Spain would almost certainly have resulted in chaos. Spain would not have been able to govern them properly. Continued misgovernment and chaos might have opened the way for forcible intervention by Germany, Japan, or France, America's commercial rivals in the Far East. The same might have occurred had the islands been turned over to the Filipinos, who were not prepared for self-government. Annexation of the entire archipelago was a solution of the problem, and it may be called a forthright and prudent act of statesmanship.[12]

Before McKinley passed from the scene a new era that would profoundly change the life of the American people was already dawning. Before the war with Spain they had lived very much within their continental domain in contented isolation. But now the United States, like the other powers, was a colonial empire in competition for the world's trade. It, too, had its island possessions, many of them distant and separated from the mainland by vast bodies of water. To protect and administer such an empire the United States would need larger armies and navies and a larger force of governing officials. It was indeed an imposing world power, and its grandeur was enough to make young Americans thrill with pride. But as yet they had not reckoned the cost of this imposing grandeur either to the taxpayer or to the individual citizen's liberties, bound to be encroached upon by increasing centralization. Did McKinley, before that tragic day at

---

[11] Olcott, Vol. II, pp. 110–11. Further comments and expressions of opinion on this incident may be had in Oberholtzer, p. 575, Millis, p. 384, and Rhodes, p. 108.

[12] For an interesting discussion of McKinley as a statesman, see H. T. Peck, *Twenty Years of the Republic*, pp. 659 ff.

Buffalo, foresee the meaning of this new era for America? Had he come to realize that, in passing from narrowed isolationism to broadening internationalism, we should need to revise our economy to fit the requirements of a new economic world order?

After his second inauguration the tone of McKinley's speeches changed perceptibly. On his tour in the South and West in the spring of 1901 he unfolded a program to promote multiplied trade relations and wider markets. At each stopping place he had a special message. At Roanoke, for example, he spoke of our growing dependence on foreign outlets for our surplus products. At Corinth, Mississippi, he once more stressed the need of securing markets for American industrial and agricultural products wherever they could be found. At Memphis the people heard him discuss the subject of markets in relation to the Open Door in China and reciprocity with Latin America.[13]

On September 5, at the Pan-American Exposition at Buffalo, McKinley delivered what may well have been his greatest public utterance. In this address to more than fifty thousand people he descanted on the place that the United States would have in the new economic world order. Instead of walling itself about with high protective-tariff barriers as before, the United States, he declared, must engage in mutual trade relations with other nations. "A system which provides a mutual exchange of commodities," he asserted, "is manifestly essential to the continued and healthful growth of our export trade. We must not repose in fancied security that we can forever sell everything and buy nothing." "The day of exclusiveness was past; protective tariffs and commercial wars no longer served their purpose. Reciprocity agreements and sensible trade arrangements should take the place of retaliatory measures. They would open up new channels for America's expanding surplus products." "If perchance," said McKinley, to the evident surprise of his audience, "some of our tariffs are no longer needed for revenue or to encourage and protect our industries at home, why should they not be employed to extend and promote our markets abroad?"[14]

---

[13] Oberholtzer, Vol. V, pp. 673–74.
[14] Olcott, Vol. II, appendix, p. 382.

This indeed sounded like a new doctrine suited to a new era, and since it came from one who had for many years consistently proclaimed the merits of the protective tariff, it must have seemed the more significant. Thus, on his final speaking tour and at his last public appearance, McKinley again revealed himself to the nation as a true statesman.[15] From McKinley the protectionist and isolationist the nation saw a new McKinley emerging —the statesman who spoke and thought in terms of a new international world order. We can only speculate what the trend and scope of his progress in that direction would have been, had McKinley been permitted to complete his second term as President.

---

[15] "He stood that day past master of the art of statesmanship" (Hay, *Memorial Address*).

CHAPTER XXII

Epilogue

On the morning of September 6, the third day that the President was to spend at the Exposition, he was scheduled to go on a sightseeing visit to Niagara Falls. On his return in the afternoon he was to hold a public reception. The reception was arranged by Secretary Cortelyou after vain attempts to persuade the President to omit it. Because of his popularity an unusually large number of people could be expected, and the strain of long standing in the receiving line and shaking hands with thousands would be very taxing. McKinley's friends were not unmindful, either, of the danger involved. Hardly more than a year before, there had been brought to light a plot to assassinate the President—the plot of a band of anarchists, in which he was the fifth of six governmental heads to be murdered.

The reception was to be held in the Temple of Music, one of the Exposition buildings, when the President's party returned from Niagara Falls. The party consisted of the President, his personal secretary Mr. Cortelyou, John B. Milburn, President of

the Exposition, and several secret-service men. A tremendous
crowd greeted them as they alighted from their carriages and
walked toward the entrance. Over the cheers and shouts of the
crowd outside could be heard the peals of the great pipe organ
from within the building. While the organist was playing the
National Anthem the President and those with him stood at attention. Then they entered the building to take a position at one
end of a long corridor. The people were admitted through a door
at the farther side and allowed to file through the corridor past
the Presidential party, going out by a door opposite the one
entered.

The President, at the head of the receiving line in conven-
tional frock coat, gray trousers, white waistcoat, and black bow
tie, began to greet his fellow countrymen with smiling face and
extended right hand. He had not been standing there long before
the black moment came. It came as suddenly and as unexpect-
edly to McKinley as it had come to Garfield and Lincoln before
him. In his behalf as in theirs, the ones charged with his safety
were insufficiently alert. Although most secret-service men and
members of the Buffalo police force had been placed on duty
as a precautionary measure, they evidently did not observe a
young man as he approached with his right hand bandaged. He
was moving along close behind the one in front of him. The
President, supposing him to have injured his right hand, reached
out to shake his left. As he did so two bullets lodged in his
body, fired from a pistol concealed beneath the bandage.

The assassin was instantly knocked to the floor, and he would
doubtless have been torn in pieces but for the President's inter-
cession.[1] He was dragged out of the building, placed in a carriage, and driven hurriedly away to escape the gathering mob.
Meanwhile the President had been lowered into a chair; he sat
waiting for an ambulance to take him to the Emergency Hospital on the Exposition grounds. An examination at the hospital
disclosed the seriousness of his wounds, one in the chest, the

---

[1] "Don't let them hurt him," the stricken President was reported to have
said to those at his side. To his secretary he said with trembling voice,
"My wife—be careful, Cortelyou, how you tell her." (Olcott, Vol. II, p. 316.)

other in the abdomen. Preparations for immediate surgery were made, and when the operation was completed the patient was taken by ambulance to the Milburn home, where the McKinleys were guests.[2]

In a short time the news was flashed over the country. Friends from far and wide hurried to Buffalo. From Washington came Vice-President Roosevelt and members of the Cabinet; from Ohio, Hanna, Day, and Herrick; from Indiana, Fairbanks. The earliest bulletins were encouraging, and they continued to be so for several days. McKinley's doctors pronounced him out of danger, and several of his friends went home. The Vice-President returned to his family in the Adirondacks.[3] Hanna, Day, and Fairbanks went to attend the G.A.R. encampment at Cleveland, which the President had planned to attend after his trip to Buffalo. The encampment, at which many veterans were present, was under the chairmanship of Hanna, who informed them in a speech of the latest bulletins from the President's sickroom. The patient, Hanna announced, was doing well. He had no pain. His pulse was normal, and he was in good spirits. The Ohio Senator's cheer was shared by Senator Fairbanks and Judge Day, both of whom addressed the gathering. An air of relief, happiness, and thanksgiving pervaded the encampment.

On the night of September 12 there was bad news from Buffalo. At Cleveland Hanna was awakened by a message about the President's suddenly critical condition. He hurried to Buffalo on a special train. Among those at the capital to receive word was Charles G. Dawes, who, with several Cabinet members, left Washington for the same destination. On the evening

---

[2] Elihu Root, McKinley's Secretary of War, maintained that his death was a direct result of propaganda published by the New York *Herald* and other Hearst papers. "What wonder," he declared, "that the weak and excitable Czolgosz answered to such impulses as these? He never knew McKinley; he had no real or fancied wrongs of his own to avenge against McKinley or McKinley's government; he was answering to the lesson he had learned, that it was a service to mankind to rid the earth of a monster; and the foremost of the teachers of these lessons to him and his kind, was, and is, William Randolph Hearst with his yellow journals" (Jessup, *Elihu Root*, Vol. II, p. 120; quoted by permission of Dodd, Mead and Company).

[3] Theodore Roosevelt, *Autobiography*, p. 349.

of that day the President's condition was thought to be so grave that members of the family and friends were summoned to his bedside. At his request Mrs. McKinley was led into the room. She sat down beside her husband, her face close to his. He smiled up at her, clasped her hand in his, and put one arm around her. Her grief was indescribable.

"I want to go too," she murmured.

To which he replied: "We are all going."

Intense as was her grief, she made no outcry. When led away, she may not have realized that this would be her last moment with her living husband. Others to see the President for the last time included his two sisters, nieces and nephews, and friends.

As they stood about his bed they heard him speak. At one time he said: "It is God's way. His will, not ours, be done." Again, his lips moved to repeat words from his favorite hymns, "Nearer, My God, to Thee" and "Lead, Kindly Light." [4]

One of the most touching incidents occurred when Mark Hanna came in to see his dying friend. When told that the President had inquired about him he seemed deeply affected. Standing at the bedside of the almost unconscious man, Hanna gave him a long, loving look, and then broke down with a heart-rending sob: "William, William, don't you know me?" [5]

Only once, it seemed, was the President in pain. He reached out a hand to Dr. Rixey and spoke as if in distress. After midnight his breathing became labored and audible. About two o'clock he stopped breathing entirely for a moment, then drew his last breath. Dr. Rixey put a stethoscope to his chest, listened, and pronounced him dead. "The great life was ended," Dawes later recorded in his diary. "The little group around him passed out. It was thus that I looked upon him last. He died as he lived,

---

[4] In his *Journal,* Dawes, after his return to Washington, named those in the sickroom when he was present. Besides Mrs. McKinley there were the President's two sisters, Mrs. Duncan and Helen McKinley; Sallie Duncan and Mary Barber, nieces; Jim McKinley and William Duncan, nephews; and a sister-in-law, Mrs. Abner McKinley. Those who were not of the family were Dr. Rixey, the attending physician, Cortelyou, two nurses, and Dawes. (*Journal,* pp. 280–81.)

[5] White, pp. 185–86.

in fear of his God and in his faith in His mercy and goodness." [6]

On the evening of September 14, the day of McKinley's death, Vice-President Roosevelt arrived in Buffalo and took the oath of office as President. During late afternoon of the previous day as he was descending Mount Tahawus in the Adirondacks, a guide had brought him a telegram telling of the President's critical condition and summoning him to Buffalo at once. Darkness came on before he and the guide could get to the clubhouse at which he had stayed. A hurried drive in a two-horse wagon over a rough wilderness road got him at dawn to the nearest railway station, forty to fifty miles away. There he learned of the President's death. A special train stood waiting to take him to Buffalo.[7]

On Sunday, September 15, the first of several funeral services was held at the Milburn house. The new President and members of the Cabinet and others attended. In a room adjoining the one in which they sat beside the casket were the family. At the close of the ceremony the body was taken to the City Hall, where it lay in state during the afternoon and evening. A great concourse thronged the building. Dawes estimated that more than ninety thousand passed by the casket. The next morning the funeral train started for Washington. It was a somber and sorrowful return. At town after town people stood along the tracks as the train passed by. Bells tolled, flags were lowered. Schoolchildren sang the departed President's hymns. At Harrisburg and Baltimore, where enormous crowds waited, bands played "Nearer, My God, to Thee" and "Lead, Kindly Light." [8]

Arrived at Washington, Dawes, who had been on the train, went to the White House, where he met his wife and the wives of several Cabinet members who were there to witness the sad homecoming. On the next morning the body was viewed by thousands as it lay in state in the rotunda of the Capitol. A brief and simple funeral service was held in the rotunda, at which the favorite hymns of President McKinley were sung and a short

---

[6] Dawes, p. 281 (quoted by permission of Dawes' executor).

[7] Roosevelt, p. 349.

[8] Dawes, pp. 282–83.

sermon was delivered by Bishop Edward G. Andrews of the Methodist Episcopal Church, an intimate friend of the McKinleys.[9] Dawes, who was present, mentioned that among the distinguished ones attending were President Roosevelt and former President Cleveland.

On the evening of September 17 the train bearing the President's body left Washington for the final resting place in Canton. It passed through Pittsburgh, where, to judge by the masses at the railroad station, the entire city had turned out to do the martyred President honor. Arrived in Canton, the body was allowed to lie in state in the City Hall. Canton was packed with friends from near-by places who, like the townspeople, had known the McKinleys for years. The Daweses, who were guests of Judge and Mrs. Day, and Senator Atlee Pomerene accompanied the Days and other friends to the McKinley home to look at the still form for the last time. Then they followed the hearse to the Methodist Episcopal Church to attend an impressive service conducted by the pastor, the Reverend C. E. Manchester. It was an occasion made noteworthy by the presence of many persons of distinction, including President Roosevelt.[10] After the ceremony there was the solemn procession to the cemetery for the final interment, and the casket was placed in a vault. The Dawes journal notes that Mrs. McKinley, bowed under her burden of sorrow, was present neither at the church service nor at the last burial rites; she remained in seclusion at the McKinley home.

While the American people were thus paying their respects to the martyred President evidence poured in of the esteem in which he was held the world over. Messages of condolence and sympathy came from the four corners of the globe. Memorial services and exercises were held in England and in many parts of the British Empire. In Europe the rulers of Germany, Russia, Austria, France, Belgium, Denmark, and Italy paid special tribute to the American President. In the Far East the Empress Dowager

[9] Olcott, Vol. II, pp. 327–28.
[10] Dawes, pp. 283–84.

of China acknowledged the good-will gesture made to her country by the United States just after the recent Boxer Rebellion. From the Philippines flowed abundant expressions of appreciation for what the McKinley administration had done to awaken among the Filipinos an abiding faith in American democracy.[11]

[11] Olcott, Vol. II, pp. 329 ff.

Bibliography

GENERAL REFERENCES

Alger, R. A. *The Spanish-American War,* 1901.

Andrews, E. B. *History of the Last Quarter Century,* 2 vols., 1896.

Bowers, R. D. *Inaugural Addresses of the Presidents,* 1929.

Bristow, J. L. *Fraud and Politics at the Turn of the Century,* 1952.

Bruce, H. A. *McKinley and the Trans-marine Possessions,* 1909.

Chadwick, F. E. *Relations of the United States and Spain (Diplomatic),* 3 vols., 1909-11.

Colman, E. M. *White House Gossip,* 1927.

Cushman, C. R. *Memorial Addresses on Lincoln, Garfield and McKinley,* 1903.

Dewey, D. R. *National Problems* (Vol. XXIV of the *American Nation* series), 1907.

Dunn, A. W. *From Harrison to Harding,* 2 vols., 1922.

Flynn, J. T. *Men of Wealth,* 1941.

Hicks, J. D. *The American Nation: History of the United States From 1865 to the Present,* 2d ed., 1949.

Jordan, P. D. *Ohio Comes of Age, 1873-1900* (Vol. V of *History of the State of Ohio,* edited by Carl Wittke), 1943.

Kennan, G. F. *American Diplomacy, 1900-1950,* 1952.

Latané, J. H. *America as a World Power* (Vol. XXV of the *American Nation* series), 1907.

Lodge, H. C. *War With Spain,* 1899.

Long, J. D. *The New American Navy,* 1903.

Millis, Walter. *The Martial Spirit,* 1931.

Oberholtzer, E. P. *History of the United States Since the Civil War,* Vol. V: *1888-1901,* 1937.

Peck, H. T.   *Twenty Years of the Republic, 1885-1905,* 1905-6.

Powers, S. L.   *Portraits of a Half Century,* 1925.

Prindiville, Kathleen.   *First Ladies,* 1941.

Reid, Whitelaw.   *Ohio in the War, Her Statesmen, Generals and Soldiers,* 2 vols., 1868.

Rhodes, J. F.   *The McKinley and Roosevelt Administrations, 1897-1909,* 1922.

Richardson, J. D., ed.   *Letters and Papers of the Presidents, 1789-1901,* Vols. XIII and XIV, 1897-1901.

Roosevelt, Theodore.   *The Rough Riders,* repr. 1925.

Smith, J. P., ed.   *Speeches and Addresses of William McKinley, From His Election to Congress to the Present Time,* 1893.

———.   *Speeches and Addresses of William McKinley, March 1, 1897, to May 30, 1900,* 1900.

Sparks, E. E.   *National Development* (Vol. XXVIII of the *American Nation* series), 1907.

Taussig, F. W.   *Tariff History of the United States,* 1923.

White, W. A.   *Masks in a Pageant,* 1928.

BIOGRAPHY

Beer, Thomas.   *Hanna,* 1929.

Burr, F. A., and R. J. Hinton.   *Life of General Philip Sheridan,* 1888.

Burton, T. E.   *Sherman,* 1906.

Caldwell, R. G.   *J. A. Garfield,* 1931.

Croly, Herbert.   *M. A. Hanna,* 1912.

Dennett, Tyler.   *John Hay,* 1934.

Eckenrode, H. J.   *R. B. Hayes,* 1930.

Jessup, P. C.   *Elihu Root,* 2 vols., 1938.

Kerr, W. S.   *Life of John Sherman,* 2 vols., 1908.

McCaleb, W. F.   *Theodore Roosevelt,* 1931.

Mott, T. B.   *Myron T. Herrick,* 1929.

Nevins, Allan.   *Henry White: Thirty Years of American Diplomacy,* 1930.

Olcott, C. S.   *Life of William McKinley,* 2 vols., 1916.

Porter, R. P.   *Life of William McKinley,* 1896.

Pringle, H. F. *Theodore Roosevelt,* 1931.

Russell, H. B. *Lives of William McKinley and Garret A. Hobart,* 1896.

Thayer, W. R. *Life and Letters of John Hay,* 2 vols., 1915.

Walters, Everett. *J. B. Foraker* (Vol. I of the *Ohio Governors* series), 1948.

Williams, C. R. *Life of R. B. Hayes,* 2 vols., 1914.

AUTOBIOGRAPHY, MEMOIRS, DIARIES, LETTERS

Cox, J. M. *Journey Through My Years,* 1946.

Dawes, C. G. *Journal of the McKinley Years,* 1950.

Depew, C. M. *My Memories of Eighty Years,* 1924.

Dewey, George. *Autobiography,* 1913.

Foraker, J. B. *Notes of a Busy Life,* 2 vols., 1916.

Hayes, R. B. *Diary and Letters of R. B. Hayes,* 5 vols. edited by C. R. Williams, 1922.

Hoar, G. M. *Autobiography of Seventy Years,* 1906.

Kohlsaat, H. H. *From McKinley to Harding: Personal Recollections of Our Presidents,* 1923.

Roosevelt, Theodore. *An Autobiography,* repr. 1929.

Schurz, Carl. *Reminiscences,* 3 vols., 1909.

Schley, W. S. *Forty-five Years Under the Flag,* 1904.

Sheridan, P. H. *Personal Memoirs,* 3 vols., 1888.

Sherman, John. *Recollections of Forty Years,* 1895.

Stoddard, H. L. *As I Knew Them: Presidents and Politics From Grant to Coolidge,* 1927.

Thompson, C. W. *Presidents I've Known,* 1929.

White, A. D. *Autobiography,* 2 vols., 1907.

Wise, J. S. *Recollections of Thirteen Presidents,* 1906.

PUBLIC RECORDS

Congressional Record, 1877-90, 1897-1901.

Important Acts of Congress in Select Statutes of the United States, 1861-1898 (compiled by W. MacDonald), 1903.

Messages and Documents, 1898-99 (abridgement in 4 vols. of documentary history of war with Spain), 1899.

Supplement to the Revised Statutes of the United States:
  Vol. I: *Forty-third to Fifty-first Congress, 1873-91,* 2d ed., 1891.
  Vol. II, No. 1-5: *Fifty-second and Fifty-third Congress, 1891-95,* 1895.
  Vol. II, No. 7: *Fifty-fourth Congress, 1895-97,* 1898.
  Vol. II, No. 8: *Fifty-fifth Congress, 1897-99,* 1899.
  Vol. II, No. 9: *Fifty-sixth Congress, 1899-1901,* 1901.

NEWSPAPERS

The Boston *Herald* was inclined to be jingoistic and war-spirited during the Spanish-Cuban crisis.

The Boston *Transcript,* the opposite, supported McKinley in the Cuban crisis and favored non-intervention.

The Chicago *Times-Herald* backed McKinley and the gold standard.

The Chicago *Tribune* was very war-spirited during the prewar months of the McKinley Presidency.

The Cincinnati *Commercial Tribune,* a merger of the *Commercial Gazette* and the *Tribune* that had begun supporting McKinley for President in 1896, in general sided with the McKinley administration.

The New York *Journal* supported Bryan for President in 1896 and 1900; a sensationalist paper, it called for war with Spain and for Cuban independence.

The New York *World* joined the *Journal* in sensational exploitation of the Cuban crisis and the war with Spain.

The New York Times, on the other hand, a politically conservative paper, supported the McKinley administration.

The St. Louis *Post-Dispatch* backed Bryan for President in both campaigns.

MANUSCRIPTS

"The McKinley Papers" in the Division of Manuscripts, the Library of Congress.

Index

Aguinaldo, leads Philippine insurrection, 134; wages guerrilla war, 152; President of Philippine republic, 134; capture, 153

Alger, R. A., appointed secretary of war, 100; public criticism, 101, 135–36; favorable report on by investigating commission, 136; dismissed, 137

Anglo-American alliance proposed, 161–62

Ballot-box forgery case, 64

Blaine, J. G., secretary of state, 55; nominated for President (1884), 72; sentiment for his nomination (1888), 74; withdrawn as candidate,76

Boxer revolt, 163

Bryan, W. J., free-silver campaign (1896), 91; defeated, 94; renominated on free-silver plank (1900), 174; for Philippine independence, 176; again defeated, 181

Cervera's fleet, under blockade in Santiago Harbor, 128; its destruction, 132

Cleveland, Grover, on the surplus, 49; on the tariff, 50; his Cuban policy, 111

Cuba, riots, 114; relief, 113; debt, 141; rehabilitation, 149; constitution, 150

Davis, Kushman, chairman of Senate Foreign Relations Committee, member American Peace Commission, 139; favors annexing Philippines, 139

Dawes, C. G., promotes McKinley candidacy, 85, 186n; appointed Comptroller of Currency, 186n; on McKinley's social life, 186–87; at McKinley's death, 202; attends McKinley burial services, 202

Day, W. R., Assistant Secretary of State, 99; made Secretary of State, 103; heads American Peace Commission, 139; reluctant about Philippine annexation, 139; for taking Luzon only, 141; against demanding Philippines on basis of conquest, 142

Debates in Senate on peace treaty, 144–45

Dewey, Admiral George, makes ready to attack Manila, 127; captures Manila, 134

Dingley tariff, 106–7

Elections of 1890, 58, 70; election of 1896, 94; election of 1900, 181

Farmer's Alliances, 61

Foraker, J. B., candidate for governor, 70; delegate-at-large at Republican National Conventions, 71, 73, 86; elected governor, 72; backs Sherman for President, 73; backs McKinley for governor, 64; defeated for United States Senate, 99n; backs McKinley for President, 85; favors intervention in Cuba, 117; Foraker Porto Rican Act, 152

Frye, W. P., member of Senate Foreign Relations Committee, 139; on American Peace Commission, for annexing the Philippines, 139

Gold Standard Act, 100

Gray, Senator George, member Peace Commission, opposes Philippine annexation, 139, 141n

Halstead, Murat, editor of Cincinnati *Commercial Gazette*, on failure of Sherman candidacy, 77; for McKinley for President, 75

Hanna, M. A., backs McKinley for governor, 63; delegate-at-large at the Republican National Conventions, 1884 and 1888, 71; favors Sherman for President, 77; becomes McKinley's political mentor, 78; gets him before public as presidential timber, 80; actively promotes his candidacy, 83–84; delegate-at-large in Republican National Convention (1896), 86; works for gold standard, 89; as campaign manager, 92–93; aspires to senatorship, 96; appointed to Sherman's vacant seat, 99n; opposed to war, 116; votes for Porto Rican Tariff, 152n; writes trust plank for Republican platform (1900), 168; fights against Roosevelt for Vice-Presidency, 171; as campaign speaker, 177–79; promotes campaign (1900), 179; chairman of G.A.R. encampment, 201; present at McKinley's deathbed, 202

Harrison, Benjamin, backed by Senators Elkins and Platt, 76; nominated for President (1888), 76; renominated (1892), 79

Hawaii, annexation, 155–56; organized as a territory, 156

Hay, John, succeeds Day as Secretary of State, 103; his instructions to American Peace Commission, 141–42; negotiates first Hay-Pauncefote Treaty, 160; offers resignation, not accepted, 160; second Hay-Pauncefote Treaty, 160–61; his Open Door policy, 163; circular note, 163–64; fearful of Republican victory (1900), 175n; his Memorial Address on McKinley, 192n; on McKinley's character, 192

Hayes, R. B., commands twenty-third Ohio volunteers, 21; commands second division of General Crook's army, 25; elected governor, 30; re-elected, 31–32; declared elected over Tilden, 35; his stand on Southern reconstruction, 35–36; Hayes' views on civil service and currency, 36–37; vetoes Bland-Allison bill, 37

Insular cases, 156–57

Lawton, General H. W., in Cuba, 131; in the Philippines, 153

MacArthur, General Arthur, in the Philippines, 153; military governor of Philippines, 153

McKinley, Mrs. Ida Saxton, before marriage, 182; marriage, 183; loss of children, 183; becomes invalid, 183–84; married life, 185–86, 187; active in Washington social life, 186–87

McKinley, William, ancestry, 13–15; youth, 16–19; enlists in Company E, Twenty-third Ohio volunteers, 20–21; at Carnifax Ferry and Antietam, 21–22; commissioned, 22–24; in battles of Kernstown, Opequam, Fisher's Hill and Cedar Hill, 23–26; commissioned brevet major, 27; prepared for law, 29; states attorney, 30–31; coal-miner case, 32–33; elected to Congress, 33–34; votes for Bland-Allison bill, 37; speech on Wood tariff bill, 40–42; re-elected, 43; on Ways and Means Committee, 44; favors tariff commission, 44–45; speech on Morrison tariff bill, 46–47; speech on Mills bill, 51–53; chairman of Ways and Means, 54; speech on McKinley tariff, 55–57; defeated for re-election, 57; elected governor, 65; legislation while governor, 65, 68; financial aid, 67; saved from bankruptcy, 81; hard times, 66–67; delegate-at-large in Republican National Convention (1884), 71; favors Blaine's nomination, 71; refuses nomination, 74–75; becomes presidential possibility, 79–80; loyalty to Harrison, 80; nominated for President (1896), 87; accepts gold standard, 89; front-porch speeches, 92–93; elected, 94; chooses Cabinet, 96–103; use of Presidential patronage, 104–5; first inaugural address, 105–6; Cuban peace policy, 112–13; its failure, 114–15; recommends war, 120; criticized for going to war, 121–22; calls for volunteers, 125–26; favors Cuban campaign, 126; demands unconditional surrender of Santiago, 133; favors holding Manila, 134; demands all of Philippines, 142; his proclamation ending war, 134–35; Philippine policy, 154–55, 177, 195–96; Porto Rican policy, 151; appoints Taft Commission, 153; favors Hawaiian annexation, 155; appoints Walker Commission, 159; opposes Anglo-American alliance, 161–62; favors Open Door in China, 163; favors American relief expedition, 164; renominated, 171; not active in 1900 campaign, 177; re-elected, 181; marriage, 182; devotion to invalid wife, 183–85; personal appearance, 191; not imperialistic, 194; as statesman, 196, 198; address at Buffalo, 197; shot at Buffalo, 200; death, 201–3; memorial services for, 203–4; tributes to, 204–5

Maine disaster, 115
Miles, General Nelson, proposes Cuban military campaign, 126; campaign in Porto Rico, 133–34; canned-meat charges, 136
Montauk Point, 135

New South, 58
New West, 59

Open Door in China, 162–63

Peace protocol, 134; peace treaty drafted, 143–44; peace treaty ratified, 147
Platt, Senator Thomas C., support of McKinley's candidacy spurned, 84; favorite son candidates, 87; schemes to make Roosevelt Vice-President, 169–70; displeased over Secretary of War Alger's dismissal, 137
Platt Amendment, 150
Populist Party, 61–62

Quay, Senator Matthew, schemes with Platt to make Roosevelt Vice-President, 170; a bitter foe of Hanna, 170n

Reid, Whitelaw, editor New York *Tribune*, member of American Peace Commission, 139; strong advocate of expansion, 139; averts breakdown of peace negotiations, 141; confident of securing a treaty, 143
Resumption Act, 31–32
Roosevelt, Theodore, made assistant Secretary of the Navy, 126–27; secret instructions to Dewey, 127; critical of McKinley, 127n; lieutenant colonel of Rough Riders, 129; protests Platt-Quay scheme, 170; ambitions to advance self, 171–72; popularity leads to nomination, 171; active in campaign (1900), 176; becomes President, 203; attends McKinley funeral services, 204
Root, Elihu, appointed Secretary of War, 137; favors sending American expeditionary troops to China, 164; on McKinley's assassination, 201n
Round Robin, 135–36

Shafter, General W. R., commands Cuban expeditionary army, 129; conducts campaign in Cuba, 130–31; proposed plan for capturing Santiago, 132–33; reports on condition of American troops, 132, 135

Sherman, John, Secretary of Treasury, 36; fails to secure Presidential nomination in 1884, 71–72; fails again in 1888, 76; re-elected Senator, 65; resigns Senate seat to become Secretary of State, 97; physical and mental impairment, 99; his resignation, 99; disappointment, 99–100
Surplus, 50, 54

Taft, W. H., heads Philippine Commission, 153; made civil governor of Philippines, 154
Tariff commission created, 44–45; reports tariff schedule, 45
Teller, Senator H. M., bolts Republican National Convention (1896), 90; author of Teller Amendment, 123

Wood, General Leonard, in Cuban War, 129; military governor of Cuba, 149